Reminiscences of a Dancing Man:

A Photographic Journey of a Life in Dance

Bill Evans

Foreword by Adrienne Clancy

National Dance Association

Associate Editors

Virginia Wilmerding, Ph.D.,
NDA Vice President of Dance Science and Somatics;
Dept. of Physical Performance and Development, University of New Mexico;
President, International Association for
Dance Medicine & Science (IADMS)

Colleen Porter Hearn
Phi Beta Kappa;
Masters in Dance Education,
George Washington University;
NDA Program Administrator

Shelby Tombras
Graduate in Dance, George Mason University
NDA Administrative Assistant

Carrie Nygard
JOPERD Associate Editor

Kelly Ferris, Brianna Kachel
SUNY Brockport

Megan Stipicevic
NDA Administrative Assistant
George Mason University

The National Dance Association (NDA) encourages authors to freely express their professional judgment through their work. Therefore, materials and terminology within this text represent the views of the author and do not necessarily reflect the position of NDA. The author's research, citations and reference structure herein do not completely follow AAHPERD publications guidelines. The author granted permission and provided all materials for publication. Copyright permission for any material that is not the original work of the author is the sole responsibility of the author and not the responsibility of NDA or AAHPERD.

Dedication

*For Don Halquist, my partner,
who helps me become a better person.*

*...I enter the dance technique studio to remind my students of their connections
to the rest of humanity, to the rest of the animal life of the planet, and to the
basic compositional elements of our universe.*

—Bill Evans,
1997 National Dance Association
Scholar/Artist Lecture:
Teaching What I Want to Learn

THE MISSION OF THE NATIONAL DANCE ASSOCIATION (NDA) IS TO INCREASE KNOWLEDGE, improve skills and encourage sound professional practices in dance education while promoting and supporting creative and healthy lifestyles through high quality dance programs.

HERALDING DANCE EDUCATORS

The National Dance Association (NDA) leads the way in dance education and recognizes Bill Evans for his lifelong contributions to our field.

BRIEF HISTORY

NDA is an association of the American Alliance for Health, Physical Education, Recreation and Dance (AAHPERD), with a spirit and purpose that were advocated by the early leaders. AAHPERD was established in 1885 and today serves almost 30,000 members. AAHPERD is comprised of six national, six district and fifty state organizations supporting the related fields. Modern dance icons like Margaret H. D'Houbler were instrumental in promoting dance education within AAHPERD and the nation. At the 1905 convention in New York City, then president Luther Halsey Gulick chose to highlight multicultural dance. Sculptor, athlete, scholar and physician, R. Tait McKenzie, captured the essence of movement in his artistic work, including the Luther Halsey Gulick Medal that is the highest AAHPERD honor. The dance section was established first in 1932 and in 1974, NDA became an association of AAHPERD.

PROGRAMS

For over 70 years, NDA has and continues to be the leader in dance education, as the founder of the national dance honor society Nu Delta Alpha, *Dance for Health!* Project, *National Standards for Dance Education* and founding member of the National Consortium of Arts Education Associations. NDA's highest honor, the Heritage Award, has been presented to such distinguished dance educators as D'Houbler, Louis Horst, Ted Shawn, Katherine Dunham, Hanya Holm and Don McKayle. Other awards recognize both professionals and students for their achievements. NDA conducts workshops and conferences throughout the United States, publishes state-of-the-art materials and advocates for quality dance programs at all levels. The National Endowment for the Arts, Harkness Foundation for Dance, Capezio BalletMakers and the U.S. Departments of Education and Humanities have all supported NDA projects.

Contents

The doctor told my mother that I would not live...
She was determined to keep me alive....

I found myself in a company of extraordinarily gifted young dancers.

It would not have occurred to me... that anyone would want to watch me for an entire evening.

...we were the most booked dance company in the United States.

Feeling alone and lost...I returned...

The cataclysmic events of September 11th made me profoundly grateful to have been able to live most of my life through the art of dance.

I encourage students to bring their senses, their feelings, their thoughts and their intuition to each facet of the dance technique class experience.

Those of us who have known Bill for half of our lives, and those who had just entered the fold, were blessed with a magical evening.

It's as if he re-thought the whole impulse toward movement for himself and arrived at some rather startling conclusions.

Foreword Honoring Bill Evans

by Adrienne Clancy

Adrienne Clancy is the Artistic Director and Founder of the exciting new dance company, ClancyWorks. She performed as a member of the Bella Lewitzky Dance Company, the Liz Lerman Dance Exchange, and as a guest artist for the Bill Evans Dance Company. Adrienne has received many awards, including the first Accomplished Graduate Award from the University of New Mexico, where she taught while earning a Masters Degree in Dance. Adrienne actively participates in helping to connect art principles with young adults and building community through various art engagement programs.

While teaching a contemporary modern dance class at a liberal arts college a few months ago, I decided to work on a tap combination. It was my silent homage to Bill Evans. When I demonstrated a rhythmic combination that seemed out of place in a modern technique class, the students thought I was joking. After the initial nervous laughter died down, I had them focus on my objectives in cross-pollinating these distinct dance forms: a way for students to apply the ease and softness of the tap rhythms in a contemporary modern combination. I found myself mouthing phrases that I first heard in Bill's class when I was a student. "Soften your sternum. Indulge in the backspace. Reach with your head. Easy knees." Over the years, these phrases have become so natural that I think of them as my own teaching techniques. But they are not purely my own, they are the echoes of a mentor. I was taught and so I teach.

I watch my students stay trapped within their comfort zones in movement. I watch them try to make the movement happen as they rely on their superficial muscles to initiate the dance sequences, as opposed to working from a sense of deep core initiation and inner connectivity to increase their range of motion. I continue to see static postures, and search for the words that can empower them to find an ease and softness simultaneously with a rhythmic clarity and elongated reach. I keep searching for the words that will connect me to them in a way that they will "get" what teachers like Bill Evans taught me when I was their age.

Now as a dance educator, I find my students captivating: young athletic bodies, earnest faces, their concentrated attention wanting so much to please, masking their fear. Any of them could easily be me, fifteen years ago, a student of Bill's trying so desperately to "get it right." I keep searching for words: "Yield to gravity. Find your sternum-pubic bone connection. Connect the rhythm to your breath. Allow yourself to soften." Soon, I see the beginning of a shift in the students, a subtle and qualitative play in the torso, the willful forcefulness of muscle-bound movement being replaced with energy at once gentler and more dynamic.

And then the moment is gone, like all dance, the most ephemeral of art forms. I am back to the tap rhythm, thinking of my own whimsical image of Bill: soft hair flying in all directions as intricate rhythms play from his feet, a dedication to committing fully to the movement without exhibiting the extent to which he is working. As a teacher, I search sometimes for his energy. His belief in the restorative and regenerative power of dance helps me, at 35, see an elongated future in dance. He was already in his fifties when I met him, and – now in his sixties – is still creating and dancing with grace and power.

What would Bill say to these students of mine? I think of his sense of play and use of wry humor in class. He called his own way of dancing through life "Evansing," recreating himself as a verb. "I suppose I must be lazy," I remember him saying of his elegant technique, where a balance of core muscles and distal-initiated movement produce a profound sense of spatial awareness and qualitative expression. "I like to expend the least amount of energy necessary to complete a task efficiently."

But lazy would be the last word that I would connect with Bill Evans. What drives Bill? Curiosity? A quest to survive artistically? A commitment to develop artists around him in order to build a healthy community for everyone? A visionary approach to link unexpected partnerships and make dance accessible to a wide audience? I think of his strengths and capabilities that took him in so many directions: his training in the Laban-Bartenieff method of movement harmony, his ability to combine dance forms from so many different cultures and genres in a cohesive manner, his articulate phrasing in both dance and writing, his generosity in sharing information and experiences, and his commitment to support the community of which he was a part. His constant pursuit to learn more about different cultures and his love of international travel – as well as his willingness to invite along students – propelled me to dance and showcase my choreography in Japan and Mexico, and inspired me to continue to pursue touring abroad. His encouragement helped me to grow confident as a dancer, choreographer, educator, writer, and now as an artistic director of my own company. His never-ending enthusiasm for art and education, as well as his passion to perform and choreograph, continues to refresh my hope in the power of dance to heal, save, and connect.

I'm back in the studio, this time with my own dance company, a hardworking group of 20 and 30-something year olds, each committed to the company's values of dance for social change, of partnering and architectural principles. I look at their eagerness to perform, their constant drive to perfect combinations, their interest to create; and I hope that I can do as I learned from Bill: inspire, develop, reinvent, and help us to survive on dance in a world that seems to want to abolish the arts. All this in a way that uses the least amount of exertion to produce an effect, so that I, too, may "Evans" my way through life elegantly and dynamically.

Adrienne Clancy (Photo by Paul Emerson)

Introduction

IN JULY OF 1997, I GAVE THE FIRST PERFORMANCES OF A SOLO SHOW I CALL *Reminiscences of a Dancing Man,* at the Rose Wagner Center for the Performing Arts in Salt Lake City, under the auspices of the Repertory Dance Theatre. I borrowed the title from a poem by the British writer Thomas Hardy.

I had been performing solo concerts regularly since 1970, when Margaret Gisolo, director of dance at Arizona State University (ASU), asked me to do so for the first time as the culminating event in a weeklong modern dance workshop that she invited me to teach. Over the past 35 years, I have performed solo concerts throughout North America, Europe, Asia and Australasia. The American Dance Festival at Connecticut College produced my first major solo show in 1976. I have celebrated many of my birthdays with solo performances, including my 45th birthday at Centre International de Danse, Paris, France, my 60th at Kenyon College in Gambier, Ohio, and my 65th at the State University of New York College at Brockport.

Beginning in 1980, my solo shows included informal chats with the audience as I changed costumes between dances. For my *Dancing Man* show in 1997 I altered that format, recording spoken information, which the audience heard as I changed costumes backstage and they viewed a series of projected images depicting significant moments from my personal and professional life journeys.

In 2004, Virginia "Ginny" Wilmerding suggested that I convert the *Reminiscences of a Dancing Man* text and slides into a book. She later asked if I would allow the National Dance Association (NDA), an affiliate of the American Alliance for Health, Physical Education, Recreation and Dance, to publish it.

Ginny danced with my professional company and worked as my colleague on the faculty of the University of New Mexico Dance Program over many years, and she is a dear friend. Since I served NDA in various capacities, including three years as a member of the board and vice president for performance, I was happy to say "Yes."

When I converted the text and slides into a book format, I found them incomplete without my dancing presence; therefore, I have extended the text and increased the number of photographic images to cover highlights of my personal and professional lives in a more comprehensive way. This is not, however, my autobiography. I hope to complete work on that project—which will tell my inner story and impart my philosophy of dance and education—within the next few years.

I have lived a complex, rich and complete life through dance, one that has been as challenging as it has been satisfying. I hope that you'll enjoy sharing some of its highlights.

–Bill Evans, August 2005

Reminiscences of a Dancing Man:
A Photographic Journey of a Life in Dance

The Early Years, 1940–1966

**Billy and Marcia Evans, backyard of
the family home in Lehi, Utah, 1949.**
Photograph by William Ferdinand Evans

James William "Billy" Evans,

nine months old.

Photograph by unknown

I WAS BORN ON APRIL 11, 1940, AT ABOUT 1:00 A.M., IN A 1939 FORD, AS MY parents traveled the 30 miles from their home in Magna, Utah (where my father worked as a boilermaker for the railroad of the Kennecott open-pit copper mine) to the Lehi Hospital. I was more than six weeks premature, weighed less than three pounds and came out feet first, before my parents (both of whom went into shock) arrived at the little country hospital. The doctor told my mother that I would not live for more than a few hours. She was determined to keep me alive, however, and stayed by my side, feeding and caring for me endlessly. By nine months—as you can see—I was fat and healthy. Mom still calls me a "miracle baby."

I started making up my own dances at age three, after seeing my first film, a Hollywood musical in which some guy (probably Fred Astaire or Gene Kelly) tap-danced. Somehow I knew immediately that I would be a dancer, and for years after that I begged my parents to let me take tap lessons. They only considered my request when the family doctor prescribed ballet classes for my sister Marcia to help strengthen her feet and ankle muscles. At the 1947 opening of the American Fork branch of the Utah Conservatory of Dance—operated by Michael and Tora DiLello, former high-wire artists for the Ringling Brothers Circus—I was awarded a scholarship of 12 free lessons for standing on my head

longer than any other child. Because there were no other boys at the audition, however, my father refused to let me accept the scholarship. I pestered him constantly after that until, in the fall of 1948, he enrolled me in the class (along with several other boys) of a retired vaudevillian hoofer who had settled in Salt Lake City and established the Purrington Academy of Dance Art. Charles Purrington, who wore a little red toupee, was 72-years old and legally blind. He would pick up our feet and move them in the appropriate patterns for the steps he wanted us to learn, and would then sit in the corner and play World-War-I-era melodies on a little spinet piano to accompany our tapping. He arranged a dance to one of those tunes, *Smile, Smile, Smile,* which Marcia and I performed at various weddings, family reunions and church socials throughout 1949 in our little hometown of Lehi, Utah, and in neighboring communities.

Billy, Marcia and Gary Evans on the front porch of the family home in Salt Lake City, 1943. Photograph by William Ferdinand Evans

This photograph shows Marcia and me with our older brother, Gary, in front of our house in Salt Lake City. The family moved here because of the poor air quality in Magna caused by the Kennecott Copper smelter. We lived here for just two years and then moved to Lehi, my father's hometown.

Here we are with our father, Ferd Evans, an elite athlete (all-conference guard for the Brigham Young University basketball team) and sportsman. After losing much of his vision to glaucoma, he quit his job as a boilermaker and opened the Evans Café on Main Street in Lehi, a Mormon village of about 3,000 people that had been known early in its history as Evansville.

Here I am at my eighth birthday party. When I wasn't dancing, I was extraordinarily shy, soft-spoken and quiet. I was a good reader and writer, but had no interest in sports. Because I didn't "fit in," I developed a vivid imagination and preferred to spend time alone in a world of make-believe.

This is a photograph of Marcia and me with our mother, Lila Snape Evans, and our baby brother, Michael, in Teton National Park in Wyoming. Our parents loved camping and fishing, and we traveled every summer to scenic spots in the intermountain west. I loved being in the great outdoors, but could not be persuaded to try fishing for more than a few minutes at a time.

Billy, Ferd and Marcia Evans on the front porch of the home of Will and Lizzy (Mary Elizabeth) Evans, Lehi, Utah, 1944.

Photograph by William Abel Evans

Billy in the front yard of our Lehi home, April 11, 1948.

Photograph by Lila Evans

Marcia, Lila, Michael and Billy Evans, 1952.

Photograph by William Ferdinand Evans

Billy and other students of June Purrington Park, my second dance teacher.
Photographs by William Ferdinand Evans

Barbara Stauffer and Billy Evans. Photograph by William Ferdinand Evans

My father had refused to let me take dancing lessons until he found a male teacher with other male students. When I took my first lesson at age eight and a half, there were several other boys in my group. I was promoted to the classes of Charles' daughter, June Purrington Park, in 1949, after which I was the only boy in my class. This photograph of *The Syncopated Clock* is from the annual Purrington/Park recital. I still have this little "Dutch boy" costume.

This is the costume I wore for *Piano Roll Blues* and *Abba Dabba Honeymoon*, both choreographed by June Purrington Park. When I received six curtain calls in the 1950 recital, at Salt Lake City's South High School, my fate was sealed. I have loved the release of endorphins and the rush of adrenaline that accompany performing ever since.

In 1951, the recital hit was *Hold Tight*, which I performed with my glamorous partner, Barbara Stauffer. The first section was "ballroom adagio," and then Barbara whipped off her skirt for the second section, which was fast, hot and rhythmic. *Hold Tight* was a current hit song by the Andrew Sisters.

In 1952, I performed a ballet for the first time. Here I am in *Rhapsody in Blue*, which, like all her choreography, was accompanied by June Purrington Park at an on-stage grand piano.

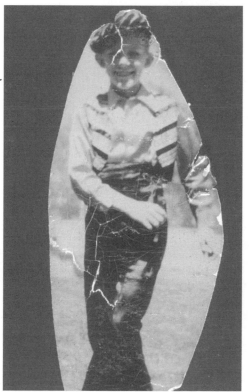

Billy in the yard of our Lehi home.
Photograph by Lila Evans

Bill, 1959.

Photograph by Arthur Gordon

In 1953, the annual family fishing vacation took us to a remote ranch near Farson, Wyoming, where we stayed with my father's second cousin and her husband, who trapped coyotes for the U.S. government throughout the Great American Desert.

This was my senior yearbook photograph. I attended the Lehi Elementary School and then the Lehi Jr./Sr. High School (both just a two-minute walk from the family home). I graduated as representative boy from junior high and as salutatorian from high school, but I was oftentimes ostracized during those six years because of my refusal to participate in sports and my insistence on performing my solo dances at school assemblies. I was a member of the Thespian Society and enjoyed performing leading roles in several school plays. I also excelled in debate, winning two state championships and one multi-state invitational competition. I was my high school's debate manager, student body business manager and yearbook business manager.

In 1959, I presented the first of five annual recitals by the Lehi-based Bill Evans School of Dance, with branches in the villages of Sandy and Draper, Utah. Here I am (page 6) in the costume my mother made for my solo to the Arabian music from the *Nutcracker*.

From 1958 through 1963, I completed two majors (English and ballet) and several concentrations (French, American history, comparative literature and Reserve Officer Training Corps) as an undergraduate student at the University of Utah. Here I am with my friend Joy, another ballet major.

Hazel Bone, Lizzy, Michael, Marcia, Billy, Will, Lila, Gary and Ferd Evans, 1953.
Photograph by Eldon Bone

Bill Evans, 1958.
Photograph by Arthur Gordon

Bill with his ballet-major-friend Joy, 1961.
Photograph by unknown

Sharon Joyce Lennberg and Bill, 1962.

Photograph by Sondra Horton (Fraleigh)

Bill Evans, Wayne Brennan, Shirley White and

Rocky Spoelstra, 1963. Photograph by unknown

Students of the Bill Evans School of Dance at the dress rehearsal

for their annual recital, Lehi High School auditorium, 1962.

Photograph by Arthur Gordon

Emily Roberts, Bill Evans, just left of center, early 1960's.

Photograph by unknown

In addition to my many other activities, from 1959 through 1963, I found time to perform with the University of Utah modern dance performing group, Orchesis, which was directed by Shirley Ririe and Joan Woodbury. Here I am in 1962 with my fiancée, Sharon Lennberg, in a work choreographed by Sondra Horton (Fraleigh), a modern dance major. I loved modern dance and I tried for one semester to make it my major, but that required me to declare a major in women's physical education with a concentration in dance. I found it extremely awkward to explain to people that I was a women's phys. ed. major, so I dropped it after one semester. Before that, I had tried majoring in engineering, architecture and secondary education. The constants throughout my five undergraduate years at the University of Utah (U of U) were courses in literature, writing, ballet and ROTC.

In 1963, as a soloist with the Utah Theatre Ballet (which later became Ballet West), I performed in Willam Christensen's *Blue Tournament*. I studied with Bill Christensen from 1955 (when I was just 15 years old) through 1963, and the imprint of his dynamic and powerful teaching lies deep within my body-mind to this day. My early exposure to Christensen, Betty Hayes, Shirley Ririe, Joan Woodbury and Virginia Tanner (all true dance pioneers at the University of Utah) taught me that I could make the seemingly impossible happen if I cared deeply enough and worked hard enough.

In the 1962 Bill Evans School of Dance recital, my brother Michael, second from the left, was among the students who performed *Ragtime Cowboy Joe*. As it turned out, this was Michael's final dance performance. When he was young, our mother worked each evening at the Evans Café, so I shared primary-care-giver responsibilities for Michael, attending to his needs from the time I arrived home from junior/senior high school until he fell asleep. He is now a commissioner (judge) with his own courtroom in Salt Lake City.

For several summers in the early 1960's, I appeared on the touring faculty of the National Association of Dance and Affiliated Artists, Incorporated (NADAA). Here I am (bottom of page 8) in a NADAA convention ballroom class in Los Angeles with my friend Emily Roberts, then a modern dance major at the University of Utah. Emily and I performed as a jazz dance duo throughout the greater Salt Lake City area from 1959 through 1961.

After graduating from the University of Utah with a ROTC commission as a second lieutenant in the United States Army, I was stationed at Fort Knox, Kentucky. After completing a tank-platoon-leader-training course, I became the printing control officer at the U.S. Army Armor School Printing Plant.

After only six weeks of active duty, I suffered an accident in an M60 tank in which my left talus (a small bone in my foot) was crushed. I suffered from *aseptic necrosis* (death without infection), meaning that the bones of my foot and ankle decalcified. This injury required me to wear a series of non-weight-bearing casts and to walk on one foot and crutches for seven and a half months. Here I am on my crutches with Sharon and Tandi.

Spending time with our daughter, Tandi (her given name is Thaïs), born on May 12, 1963 in Salt Lake City, brought joy to these otherwise difficult days.

Bill Evans and Chanson Finney, junior officers, with three senior enlisted men, 1964. Photograph by unknown

Sharon and Bill Evans with their daughter Tandi, 1963. Photograph by unknown

Bill and Tandi in front of our rented mobile home near Radcliff, Kentucky, 1963. Photograph by Sharon Evans

Bill Evans and Virginia Everett, 1964.
Photograph by unknown

Bill and Tandi, 1965. Photograph by Lila Evans

Bill Evans in *Samson and Delilah* with the Briansky Ballet, Binghamton, New York, 1966. Photograph by unknown

Bill Evans, Dolores Lipinsky, Orin Kayan and other members of the Ruth Page International Ballet, 1966. Photograph by unknown

As soon as I was able, I started dancing again, even though the Army doctors had told me that I would never regain normal use of my left ankle. Here I am in the *Snow Pas de Deux* from Fernand Nault's *Nutcracker* for the Louisville Civic Ballet in 1964. Because a tall male was then very hard to find in a regional ballet company, both Fernand and Nell Fisher (the choreographers for whom I worked in Louisville) were kind and clever enough to choreograph material for me that required minimal use of my weak and almost immobile left foot and ankle.

After only two years, Sharon and I realized that our marriage was a mistake, and she took Tandi and returned to Utah. Here I am visiting Tandi at my family's home in Lehi while on furlough from the Army.

Because I am a tall, coordinated male, I was able to find work immediately after moving to New York City in September 1965, despite the injury to my left foot and ankle. While working as an apprentice to the Harkness Ballet, I was able to participate in numerous projects for the New York City-based Oleg Briansky Ballet, the Washington D.C. Ballet, the Atlanta Ballet and other organizations.

I also danced with the Ruth Page International Ballet. Here I am in Page's *La Giara,* which starred Carla Fracci and Erik Bruhn and was performed at the Lyric Opera House in Chicago. With the Ruth Page troupe, I completed a four-month season in Chicago and then a three-month cross-country bus tour. Ruth liked my theatrical flare and strong sense of rhythm and encouraged me to stay in her troupe, in which she predicted my successful future.

The RDT Years, 1967–1974

Bill and Tandi, 1967.

Photograph by unknown

Lynn Wimmer, Joan Moon Butler and Bill Evans, 1968.

Photograph by Doug Bernstein

Bill Evans and Tim Wengerd, 1969.

Photograph by Doug Bernstein

Bill Evans and members of RDT, 1969.

Photograph by Doug Bernstein

DESPITE THE SUCCESS AND SATISFACTION I was experiencing as a New York/Chicago-based ballet dancer, the separation from my daughter Tandi was increasingly painful. In March of 1967, I returned to Utah for what was supposed to be a one-week visit. After spending time with Tandi, I decided to stay in Utah to become a weekend father and see her grow up.

I enrolled in the Master of Fine Arts program in the Department of Ballet and Modern Dance at the University of Utah, where Willam Christensen awarded me a teaching assistantship in ballet. After just one quarter of coursework, I was asked to join the Repertory Dance Theatre (RDT) by Joan Woodbury, a U of U professor of modern dance and RDT advisor. This was an extraordinary opportunity that offered me full-time employment as a professional modern dancer/choreographer as I completed the requirements for the MFA (mostly by independent study). One of the first RDT works I performed was José Limón's *Concerto Grosso*, shown here.

I found myself in a company of extraordinarily gifted young dancers, including the phenomenal Tim Wengerd, with whom I shared leading roles in John Butler's *The Initiate*, one of two original works he created for RDT. Month-long residencies by New York City-based choreographers and teachers provided unparalleled opportunities for my positive change and growth. Some of the world's most distinguished modern dance artists would attend to our artistic development all day and evening during such residencies. These artists would teach company classes, direct several hours of rehearsals during which they would create or restage choreographic work, and then mentor us at informal evening meals and gatherings.

Anna Sokolow worked with RDT on several occasions, and I developed a powerful empathy for her work and a profound respect for her artistic depth and courage. Here I am in her *Steps of Silence*, which she created for us in 1969. Sokolow became a close friend and a significant artistic mentor for me, always seeing and advising me about my work when it was performed in New York City over the following decade.

Donald MacKayle staged his work *Nocturne* on RDT and served as our company teacher on several occasions. Kay Clark and I were "artistic coordinators" for most of the seven years I spent as a full-time member of RDT. By 1968 the company had transformed to an "artistic democracy," in which each dancer had a vote on all artistic matters. The University of Utah administration demanded that we create supervisory positions and appoint company spokespersons, and Kay and I most often served in those roles, joined sometimes by Lynne Wimmer (now a professor of dance at the University of South Florida) or by Linda C. Smith (now RDT's artistic director). The company still flourishes in Salt Lake City, though it is no longer connected to the University of Utah and has had a conventional governance structure for more than two decades.

Several times a year, all interested RDT members had opportunities to create new works on company colleagues. We would then decide, by group vote, which works would receive production in formal concerts and, later, which works would enter the active repertory. Here I am with Kathy McClintock in Tim Wengerd's *Quintet*. After a few years in RDT, Tim danced for several years as the principal male dancer of the Martha Graham Dance Company in New York. He passed away in 1989 after returning to his hometown of Albuquerque, where I had the good fortune of renewing our close friendship for the final year of his life.

In my early RDT years, I was still thought of as a ballet dancer. I taught ballet-based company classes on a regular basis and appeared a few times as a guest with Ballet West. My last professional performance as a ballet dancer was in 1970, when I danced the Cavalier in *Nutcracker* for the Des Moines (Iowa) Civic Ballet.

In 1974, I completed my seventh and final year with RDT, during which we premiered José Limón's *There is a Time*. I have continued to create and restage choreographic works for RDT over the 31 years that have elapsed since my departure from the company. I still consider myself very much a part of the "RDT family."

Kay Clark, Bill Evans and Tim Wengerd, 1969.
Photograph by Doug Bernstein

Bill Evans and Kathleen McClintock, 1969.
Photograph by Doug Bernstein

Bill Evans and Raya Lee with the Des Moines Civic Ballet Company, 1970. Photograph by unknown

Bill Evans in "A Time to Kill" from José Limón's *There is a Time*, 1974. Photograph by Doug Bernstein

Left: Tim Wengerd, Gregg Lizenbery and Eric Newton in *Interim Part I*; Right: Kay Clark and Bill Evans in *Interim Part II*, 1969.

Photographs by Doug Bernstein

Karin Janke and Klaus Beelitz, of the Deutsche Oper Ballet, in *Aufbrucken*, 1969.

Photograph by unknown

Linda C. Smith and Tim Wengerd of the Repertory Dance Theatre in *When Summoned*, 1970.

Photograph by Doug Bernstein

My first significant choreographic success took place in 1969, when Walter Terry, of the *Saturday Review of Literature,* and Clive Barnes, of the *New York Times,* traveled to Salt Lake City to evaluate an RDT season. Both of those esteemed critics declared my work *Interim* to be the outstanding company-member-choreographed work. We later performed this work on several cross-country tours, where numerous other critics also praised it and stated that I was a choreographer of promise. I had never thought of myself as a particularly skilled dance maker, but these affirmations encouraged me to pursue choreography more diligently and to form a new sense of who (and what) I am.

My second significant choreographic success came in Berlin, West Germany. I was invited to Berlin to create a new work when Gert Reinholm, artistic director of the Deutsche Oper Ballet, asked Walter Terry to recommend a young American choreographer. I received more accolades for this ballet, *Aufbrucken,* than for any work I have created since. Berlin audiences and critics from throughout West Germany adored it. Solely on the basis of this one piece, I was invited by Gert Reinholm to create and direct a professional modern dance ensemble as an adjunct to the German Opera Ballet. I came very close to accepting this amazing offer, but my profound allegiance to RDT won out and I decided to remain in Utah.

I restaged *Aufbrucken,* with the English title of *When Summoned,* for RDT in 1970, and we toured it throughout the U. S., where it was well-received by audiences and critics. In this mostly abstract ballet, the men march nobly off to war in the beginning and return defeated and dying in the end. This was my anti-Vietnamese War piece, even though it was set in my imagination in ancient Sumeria. After seeing this work at Yale University, Walter Terry wrote in the *Saturday Review of Literature* that I was "one of the best choreographic forces to touch the whole American dance scene."

In the summer of 1968, I worked for six weeks as a teacher and choreographer for the Midwest Dance Camp at the University of Kansas in Lawrence. Larry Long, ballet master of the Ruth Page International Ballet, gave me this opportunity. For the concluding dance camp concert I created a piece, *Facets*, for teen-aged students (including Karole Armitage, who later rose to stardom as a partner to Merce Cunningham). On the basis of that work, I was invited by Kansas dance pioneers Elizabeth Sherbon and Alice Bauman to represent emerging choreographers at

Bill Evans at the American Dance Symposium in Wichita, Kansas, 1968; On his left are Charles Weidman and Bella Lewitzky; Fourth from his left is Alice Bauman. Photograph by unknown

their American Dance Symposium held later that summer at Wichita State University. In a lecture demonstration at that conference I shared a work called *Chairs*. This one appearance resulted in numerous invitations to complete teaching and choreographic residencies at U. S. colleges and universities, and jump-started a free-lance career that has taken me to all 50 states and many other countries, and is still thriving today.

In 1970, I choreographed one of my most enduringly popular works, *For Betty*, as a tribute to my mentor in the MFA program at the University of Utah, Betty Hayes. Betty introduced me to the work of Hanya Holm, which includes numerous movements that cycle through the vertical, sagittal and horizontal planes. I was inspired by this new awareness of spatial possibilities and by Betty's suggestion that I create a "joyful and exuberant" work to balance the numerous "heavy" works in the RDT repertory at a time of social upheaval. Each dancer must execute hundreds of leaps/hops/jumps in this 10-minute piece to a concerto grosso by Antonio Vivaldi. Over the decades, I have been asked to restage this work for numerous professional and college dance companies from coast to coast. The U of U Department of Modern Dance has asked me to restage it in 2006 for a concert honoring Dr. Hayes, who will be 94.

In 1971, I created *Tin-Tal*, a quintet for Linda C. Smith, Gregg Lizenbery, Kathleen McClintock, Manzell Senters and Karen Steele. This piece fuses African and East Indian influences with modern dance, and is set to Indian tabla music by Mahapurush Misra. My goal was to create a work that was as kinesthetically

Bill Evans, Gregg Lizenbery, Kay Clark, Lynne Wimmer, Manzell Senters and Eric Newton, in *For Betty*, created for RDT as a tribute to Elizabeth R. Hayes, 1971. Photograph by Doug Bernstein

Linda C. Smith in *Tin-Tal*, with a set by M. Kay Barrell, 1971. Photograph by Doug Bernstein

Gregg Lizenbery, Linda C. Smith, Bill Evans and Lynne Wimmer in *The Legacy*, 1972.

Photograph by Doug Bernstein

inviting as possible, and many audiences over the years have found it to be just that. I later excerpted Linda's role as a solo for myself, which I performed hundreds of times on four continents over three decades.

In 1972, I received my first substantial choreographic grant (from the Eccles Foundation) and used it to create *The Legacy* for RDT. Costumes were by Ron Hodge, our resident costume designer, and the set was by M. Kay Barrell, our resident lighting and set designer. I drew on my own Mormon background for this work, basing it on the polygamous marriages of my great-great-grandfather, Abel Evans, a Welshman who emigrated to Utah and established a household with three wives. This is the only work I have created that is completely narrative. RDT was apprehensive about performing this work in Utah, where the polygamous history of the dominant culture was sometimes a source of embarrassment. Before deciding whether or not to include it in an upcoming Salt Lake City season, I invited Virginia Tanner, the great children's creative dance pioneer, to attend a rehearsal. Virginia, a mentor to RDT, was the youngest child of the youngest wife of a well-established Mormon patriarch. She sat alone in the 1,800-seat Kingsbury Hall and watched a run-through, after which she said, with tears streaming down her eyes, "That's exactly how it was." This gave me the courage to proceed and to share it with our largely Mormon audiences. Many years later, this work inspired a book (with accompanying videotape), *The Legacy: Bill Evans Reaching Out from the Regional Southwest,* by Jennifer Allen Noyer, published in August 2000 by Harwood Academic Publishers, ISBN 90-5755-115-2 (NTSC), ISBN 90-5755-118-7 (Pal).

Later in 1972, I choreographed *Piano Rags* to the music of Scott Joplin with Joan Moon. I drew on the Vaudevillian dances I had learned from Charles Purrington as a child. We performed in front of an authentic vaudevillian-era painted backdrop donated by Salt Lake City's Capital Theatre, where it been stored and forgotten about half a century earlier. Both *Tin-Tal* and *Piano Rags* were included in our program when RDT was honored to be the second dance company (after Alvin Ailey's American Dance Theatre) to perform in the Opera House at the Kennedy Center in Washington, D.C.

Bill Evans in *Piano Rags*, 1972.

Photograph by Doug Bernstein

Bill Evans, Tandi Evans and Cynthia, in Millcreek Canyon, Utah, 1973. Photograph by Gregg Lizenbery

When Tandi was in the fourth grade, Sharon took her to Santa Barbara, where she had been offered a position teaching dance at the University of California. This separation from my daughter was agonizing for me, but I took advantage of whatever opportunities I could find to continue to be part of her life. Here we are in the summer of 1973 during one of her summer visits back to Utah. Tandi is holding my Miniature American Eskimo dog, Cynthia, named after a legendary ballerina. I had been given the puppy during a choreographic residency at American Ballet Theatre in New York City, where I created a work that Cynthia Gregory, Terry Orr and Clark Tippet performed later that summer at the Jacob's Pillow Dance Festival in Massachusetts.

Michael Evans, Bill Evans, Marcia Evans Russon and Gary Evans. Photograph by Ferd Evans

In 1974, our grandfather William Abel Evans died peacefully in his sleep at age 98. These photographs were taken after his interment at the Lehi Cemetery. Grandpa had moved into our family home after the death of our grandmother, Lizzy Evans, in 1958. Will and Lizzy had only one child, our father (Ferd), which was very unusual in the Mormon culture. Our mother, for example, was one of 12 children in the James and Viva Snape family. Mom had difficulty carrying children because of a "walled uterus," and was advised not to become pregnant, hence my premature birth. When Mom was carrying her last child, Michael, she was misdiagnosed with an abdominal tumor, and Michael came within minutes of being surgically removed before a second physician gave a correct diagnosis. She calls Mike and me her "two miracle babies."

Ferd and Lila Evans, 1974. Photograph by Bill Evans

Bill Evans and Gregg Lizenbery
in *Within Bounds*, 1973.
Photographs by Doug Bernstein

In the spring of 1973, in Seattle, RDT completed one of the first extensive residencies conducted under the Artist in the Schools Program of the National Endowment for the Arts (in which I became one of the first certified dance movement specialists). I was ill with the London flu for the entire month, but continued to teach, rehearse and perform. At all other times, I lay in my hotel bed watching televised news reports of American prisoners of war returning from Vietnam. The only view through the hotel room window was of a concrete parking structure with black metal bars at all the openings. When I returned to Salt Lake City, I worked out the frustrations caused by this "confinement" by creating *Within Bounds,* a duet with Gregg Lizenbery. It was about the horrors of war and man's inhumanity to man, but it was also an investigation of aspects of my relationship with Gregg over the six years that we had been life partners. We were able to perform this work with RDT and in free-lance engagements throughout the U.S. over many years. This piece came from deep places within us, and it was almost always met with powerful responses and standing ovations. Byron Belt of the *Long Island Press* and other syndicated Newhouse Newspapers, said, after seeing us at Hunter College Playhouse in Manhattan, that we "performed with absolute magnificence."

In April of 1973, I spent three weeks in Iowa City, where I had been commissioned to create a work for the University of Iowa's Center for New Performing Arts Dance Ensemble. I had made prior arrangements to collaborate with a composer from the University of Iowa's New Music Ensemble, but when I arrived he was so consumed by other projects that he could not honor his commitment. Dejected, I walked off campus and sat in a dingy little bar, where a Kentucky blue grass band was playing. I was taken by one of their tunes, "Hard Times," and asked if they would come over to the university the next day and record some of their music as the basis for a new choreographic work. They generously agreed to do so, and I found myself making a piece about depression-era Appalachia. In this mostly abstract piece I explored the dynamics of three people trapped in religious fundamentalism, poverty and illiteracy, and the resulting self-degradation and spousal abuse that they encounter. Like a few of my other works, it combines humor and tragedy, and some audiences laugh while others are disturbed. Often, audiences will argue at intermission about what was actually occurring. I love making such multi-layered works because they reflect

Bill Evans in *Hard Times*, 1973.
Photograph by Doug Bernstein

the reality of the life I have lived. Of the more than 200 works I have choreographed, this is one of my personal favorites, and I continued to perform it myself through age 58.

Over several months in 1973, I created a work for RDT called *Five Songs in August*, under the first of several choreographic fellowships I received from the National Endowment for the Arts. I commissioned a score from Stanley Sussman, a pianist and composer who had worked with me during the summer of 1973 in the annual six-week RDT Summer Workshop. I was especially in love with life that summer and wanted to capture my feelings of being spiritually uplifted by the beauty of the Utah mountain valleys, particularly in August. Stanley and I were inspired by the flow and dynamics of mountain streams, the shimmering of cottonwood and aspen trees in the afternoon sun, and the tremendous sense of space one experiences in the Great Salt Lake Valley. We agreed to explore five different qualities of joyful affirmation—serenely easy-going, starkly introspective, sensually luxuriant, sexually romantic and athletically exuberant—and tried to capture each of those moods in five different wordless songs. *Five Songs* crystallized the most authentic and original movement vocabulary of any piece I had made up to that point, and it became a signature work that has been performed throughout the U.S. by several companies. I have returned to the seminal movement ideas contained within it many times over the years for motifs to be explored more deeply.

In the spring of 1974, I accepted a position as assistant professor in the University of Utah Department of Ballet and Modern Dance, and made plans to conclude my seven-year membership RDT. As a goodbye gift to the company I loved so much, I created a suite of dances to music arranged and recorded by Glenn Miller and his Orchestra. I drew on memories of the Hollywood movie musicals I adored as a child in the 1940s to create an affectionate spoof, *Jukebox*, in six sections with the working titles of "Parade, Fred and Ginger, Jitterbug, Modernaires, Tennis and Apple Tree."

Top: Martin Kravitz and Linda C. Smith in the *Second Song*; Middle: Linda C. Smith and Lynne Wimmer in the *Fourth Song*; Bottom: Lynne Wimmer, Linda C. Smith and Karen Steele in the *Fifth Song*, from *Five Songs In August*, 1974.
Photographs by Ross Terry

Bill Evans in his "tennis solo" from *Jukebox*, 1974.
Photograph by David Gotwald

Audiences loved this piece and it became a staple repertory item for years after I left the company. On several occasions, RDT has asked me to come back to restage this work for a new generation of dancers.

In the fall of 1974, in addition to teaching courses in the University of Utah Modern Dance Program, I restaged one work and created another for Ballet West. Willam Christensen had been my teacher for almost eight years in the 1950s and 1960s and I was honored to work for the company he founded during the last year of his artistic directorship. I worked harder on this commission than on any other before or since, with extensive daily rehearsals over six weeks. Willam

Members of Ballet West in *Echoes of Autumn*, 1975 (center/standing, Cynthia Young; far right Tomm Ruud and Victoria Morgan).
Photograph by unknown

and Bené Arnold (his ballet mistress) were very supportive of my exploration and even invited me to teach regular (modern) company classes. I felt that this work was exquisitely crafted and that the leading dancers, Cynthia Young, Tomm Ruud and Victoria Morgan, mastered my fluid, three-dimensional modern dance vocabulary brilliantly. Mr. Christensen described it as "poetic." Unfortunately, the work did not remain for long in the Ballet West repertoire, because, as is often the case in repertory companies, it was difficult for the dancers to maintain the subtleties of a new vocabulary once the choreographer was no longer available to direct rehearsals.

Solo Concerts and Free-Lance Gigs, 1970–2005

Bill Evans in posed moment from
José Limón's *A Time to Kill,* Cleveland,
Ohio, 1974.
Photograph by David Gotwald

Bill Evans in posed moment from *Five Songs in August***, Cleveland, Ohio, 1974. Photograph by David Gotwald**

In 1970, I was invited to teach a one-week summer workshop in modern dance technique, composition and improvisation at Arizona State University (ASU) in Tempe. I was also asked to perform a solo concert. Margaret Gisolo, director of the ASU Dance Program and an extraordinary human being in many ways, had seen my presentation at the 1968 American Dance Symposium in Wichita and had decided that I could accomplish such an assignment. It would not have occurred to me to seek such an engagement or that anyone would want to watch me for an entire evening. However, I was excited and flattered by the invitation and accepted it. This began a solo-performing career that has lasted for 35 years and represents one of the most satisfying and productive facets of my life's work. Margaret Gisolo is the same age as my

Photograph by John Brandon (1975)

Mom and she became a kind of "artistic mother" to me. For 15 years, she and her successor, Beth Lessard, continued to invite me to ASU to teach, perform and choreograph. I am eternally indebted to them both for their mentorship, their friendship and their faith in me.

The following pages contain solo photographs taken over a period of more than 30 years.

Immediately after leaving RDT, I served as artistic advisor to the Fairmount Dance Theatre in Cleveland, Ohio, where I met an incredibly talented young lighting designer, David Gotwald, with whom I collaborated over the next several years on many different projects. For two years, I commuted frequently between Salt Lake City and Cleveland, teaching the young Fairmount dancers and setting several works on them, including *For Betty, Tin-Tal, Hard Times, Within Bounds* and *Five Songs in August.* The photograph on page 21 has become a signature image of me, appearing on hundreds of posters, flyers and other promotional materials.

Photograph by David Gotwald (1977)

The photographs on this page show me in *Tin-Tal* at age 35 and *Dallas Blues* at age 37. I performed *Tin-Tal* in hundreds of solo concerts between 1971 and 2003. Hubert Saal called it a "perceptively observed religious ritual" in *Newsweek* magazine in 1972. The American Dance Festival, then in residence at Connecticut College, commissioned *Dallas Blues*, which commemorates the life of my former RDT colleague Manzell Senters, who died tragically in 1974.

In 1978, I visited the New York City studios of the famous dance photographer Jack Mitchell. The first of these photographs captures a moment from a technique class combination on which I was then working. The second is a moment from the *Fifth Song in August*. The third image is a "mug shot" that I used in press packets for the next several years.

To celebrate my 41st birthday, I performed two different solo concerts at the University of Washington in Seattle on April 10 and 11, 1981. On the second evening, I performed my version of Morton Gould's *Tap Dance Concerto*, accompanied by a full symphony orchestra in the pit, conducted by Joseph Levine. On page 25 are four photographs from those concerts. The first two show me in the formal attire I wore for the *Tap Dance Concerto*. The third is from Matt Mattox's *Opus Jazz Loves Bach* and the fourth is from *El Bailador*, choreographed for me by the prominent Pacific Northwest flamenco artist Teodoro Morca.

Photographs by Jack Mitchell (1978)

Matt Mattox was one of my favorite teachers during the year I spent studying at Harkness House for Ballet Arts in New York City, where he taught classes in both jazz technique and Cechetti-style ballet. I invited Mattox to create a work for RDT in 1973, and when I formed my own company in 1975 he gave us unlimited rights to perform that work. I still perform a solo version of it some 31 years later. Teo Morca became my friend during the years I lived in Seattle, when my company completed numerous residencies at Western Washington University in Bellingham, where Teo had a school and company. I had studied Spanish dance as a teen with June Purrington Park and as an undergraduate student with Willam Christensen. Teo graciously created a work for me based on what I remembered from those long-ago experiences.

The photograph on page 26 is of *Sweet and Lovely*, which I choreographed to a recording made for me by jazz pianist Bill Evans.

Bill Evans in two moments from his choreography of the *Tap Dance Concerto*, and one each from Matt Mattox's *Opus Jazz Loves Bach* and Teodoro Morca's *El Bailador*. Photographs by Kurt Fischer (1981)

Bill Evans in *Sweet and Lovely.*

Photograph by Jack Mitchell (1981)

Photograph by Jack Mitchell (1981)

In 1981, Jack Mitchell photographed me again. This time it was at the request of Willam Como, editor-in-chief of *Dance Magazine (DM)*, who had decided to publish a feature article on me after seeing my 41st birthday solo concert in Seattle. This shot from my solo *Tin-Tal* was originally intended for the *DM* cover. As often happens, plans changed and the cover article was shelved. Instead, *DM* ran a shorter feature about me using another of Mitchell's photographs.

On page 28 is one of my favorite photographs, for many reasons. First, I like its composition. Second, it captures the pervading sense of loneliness I experience as a solo free-lance artist spending so much time away from home. Third, it reminds me of one of the most supportive and influential people in my life, Janyce

Bill Evans in the studio of the Warren Civic Ballet, Warren, Ohio.

Photograph by Rick Murdoch (1982)

life, Janyce Hyatt. Jan coordinated my visit to the Warren Civic Ballet as part of a residency she arranged at Allegheny College in Meadville, Pennsylvania. She first saw me perform in 1974, in Cleveland, Ohio. Almost immediately, she began inviting me to teach, perform and choreograph in her "little corners of the world"—first at the Ashtabula, Ohio, Arts Center and then at Allegheny College. Between 1975 and 2004, Jan produced more than 20 of my solo or company residencies. Her belief in me and my work, and her mentorship, have made a tremendously positive difference in my life. In June of 2004, I was able to perform at Allegheny College just before she retired from her position as director of dance studies. I closed that performance with a solo dedicated to her as a token of appreciation for all she had given me over these many years.

During a 1985 solo residency at Allegheny College, Bill Owens photographed me in moments from: a) *Alternating Current*, b) *Jazz Three Ways*, and c) *Soliloquy*.

I choreographed *Alternating Current* in 1982 for Jim Coleman and Terese Freedman as they left my Seattle-based troupe and started their own duet company. Later, I performed it dozens of times with such stunning artists as Gregg Lizenbery, Karen Unsworth, Debra Knapp and Candace Earnest.

I learned *Jazz Three Ways* from Daniel Nagrin in 1980, when he taught in my Seattle Summer Institute of Dance and appeared as a guest with my company. I had the honor of performing this suite of jazz-inspired modern dances over the next several years. More significantly, the time I spent with Daniel provided guidance that I had sorely needed. Daniel was 64 when he taught me these dances, and he served as a powerful role model for me, illustrating that a dancer could still be a mesmerizing presence at that age. In the many talks we had before and after classes and rehearsals, he shared stories of his life as a performer, teacher, choreographer and company director. I still draw upon his wisdom 24 years later. In April of 2002, *Dance Magazine* published my short tribute to this legendary artist.

Soliloquy is a solo I made for myself to the music of Bill Evans the jazz pianist in 1985. It allowed me to crystallize the finest dancing I ever did, as I reached my physical and expressive zeniths as a performing artist between ages 45 and 55. Daniel Nagrin, who told me in 1985 "I wasn't old, just lazy," pushed me into creating a conditioning program for myself (running and weight lifting) and improving my diet and nutrition. I was amazed to find myself becoming technically stronger at an age when many of my dancing peers were deciding to retire from performing. I am forever grateful to Daniel for "kicking my butt" at precisely the right time.

In 1985, I served as guest artist in the Department of Modern Dance at the University of Utah for one

Photographs by Bill Owens (1985)

academic quarter. During that time I restaged *For Betty* for the student Performing Danscompany and performed three solo concerts. *For Betty* was selected that year for a gala concert at the National American College Dance Festival at the Kennedy Center in Washington D.C. My solo concerts included *Tin-Tal* and the world premiere of *Dances for My Father,* a suite of tap dances to music arranged and recorded by "Count" Basie and His Orchestra. I have performed *Dances for My Father* hundreds of times over the years, but one of the most satisfying experiences occurred in Perth, Australia, where Vicky Fairfax, of the *West Australian*, described my performance as follows:

> In this homage, his feet tap out a strong musical rhythm while the rest of his body seems to be listening and then responding with its own dance, as though the music of the feet has stirred strong memories. His head tilted, his shoulder curling, he seems to be occasionally recalling some past regret. It is a virtuoso performance.

In 1986, I performed a series of solo concerts at Indiana University in Bloomington, where I had just become the director of modern dance. I think that this photograph captures the strength, health and love of life I was then experiencing.

Bill Evans in *Tin-Tal* and *Dances For My Father*.

Photographs by John Brandon (1985)

Photograph courtesy of the Indiana University News Bureau (1986)

In 1989, Santa Fe photographer Jane Mont captured these moments from my solo *Soliloquy* during my first year as a resident of New Mexico. In 1994, I performed as a soloist in the full-length version of my work, *Velorio: A Vigil for the Deceased*, produced by dear friend Shirley Jenkins at the University of Washington's Meany Hall in Seattle. I choreographed *Velorio* to express the overwhelming sadness I had experienced during the late 1980s and early 1990s when beloved friends, including Tim Wengerd, Woody McGriff and Daniel Chick, died of AIDS. Shirley Jenkins gave me the opportunity to stage this work for 17 dancers, a 50-person chorus, and a 16-person orchestra.

Bill Evans in performance shot from *Velorio*.
Photograph courtesy of Strong Wind, Wild Horses (1994)

Bill Evans in studio shots from *Soliloquy*.
Photographs by Jane Mont (1989)

Above: Bill Evans in *Albuquerque Love Song*

Left: Bill Evans in *Saintly Passion.* Photographs by Pat Berrett

Bill Evans in *Tin-Tal.* Photograph
by Pat Berrett

Albuquerque dance photographer Pat Berrett captured hundreds of images of my choreographic works in performance over a period of almost 15 years. On this page you see me in three concerts given at the University of New Mexico's Rodey Theatre: a) *Albuquerque Love Song,* to a commissioned score by Michael Cava, 1997; b) *Saintly Passion,* to an aria from Bach's *St. Matthew Passion,* 1999; and c) *Tin-Tal,* to music by Mahapurush Misra, also 1999.

Bill Evans Dance Company, 1975–1983

Members of the Bill Evans Dance Company—
David Gotwald (lighting designer/production
manager), Peggy Hackney, Jim Coleman, Regina
DeCosse, Gregg Lizenbery, Erik Whitmyre and Shirley
Jenkins, Seattle, 1977. Photograph by Bill Evans

Bill Evans in *Five Songs in August.* Photograph by John Brandon (1975)

Bill Evans, Ann Asnes and Gregg Lizenbery in *Hard Times*. Photograph by John Brandon (1975)

IN THE SUMMER OF 1975, WHILE WORKING AS AN ASSISTANT PROFESSOR IN THE University of Utah Department of Modern Dance, I formed the Bill Evans Dance Company. Our first engagement was a four-week residency at the American University/Wolf Trap Academy of Performing Arts in Washington, D.C. Our premier performances were given in the National Cathedral, for over 2,000 people in two evenings. Dancers included Gregg Lizenbery, Shirley Jenkins, Ellen Bryson, Donna White and Phyllis Haskell. Our second engagement was in the Utah Bicentennial Celebration of Dance, at Kingsbury Hall, University of Utah, where we performed along with Ballet West, RDT and Ririe-Woodbury Dance Company. For this very special occasion, Gregg Lizenbery, Ann Asnes and I performed my work *Hard Times*. It so happened that dozens of American dance presenters were in Utah at that time, attending a conference organized by the National Endowment for the Arts (NEA). On the basis of that one performance, I received a Guggenheim Fellowship, my new company received numerous touring engagements, and we were asked by Charles Reinhart to be resident company at the American Dance Festival in New London, Connecticut for six weeks in the summer of 1976.

In 1976, while touring almost non-stop throughout several regions of the United States, the Bill Evans Dance Company moved its base from Salt Lake City to Seattle. A well-established non-profit organization, Dance Theatre Seattle, invited me to bring my whole company to the Pacific Northwest, to take over the Dance Theatre School and establish regular performance seasons. The February 1977 issue of *Dance Magazine* included a feature story on my life in dance and my move to Seattle. The photograph on page 33 shows most of the 1977-1978 Bill Evans Dance Company. I met our lighting designer, David Gotwald, when I served as artistic advisor to the Fairmount Dance Theatre in Cleveland. Peggy Hackney joined my company after we both taught in the summer of 1976 at the American Dance Festival. Jim Coleman, Regina DeCosse, Erik Whitmyre and Shirley Jenkins had all been modern dance majors at the University of Utah when I taught there full-time from 1974 to 1976. Upon graduation from the University of Utah, they moved to Seattle to work full-time for my company and school.

Members of the Bill Evans Dance Company—Bill Evans, Mary Fain (guest artist), David Gotwald, Gregg Lizenbery, Shirley Jenkins, Teo Morca (guest artist), David Sannella, Erik Whitmyre, Debbie Poulsen, Joanna Mendl Shaw, Thom Gruenwald, Wade Madsen, Shannon Gordon, Daphne Lowell and Jim Coleman, Bellingham, WA, 1978.
Photograph by Daniel Chick.

Gregg Lizenbery and Peggy Hackney in rehearsal for *The Legacy,* **Dance Theatre Seattle.**

Photograph by Carol Beech (1977)

Almost immediately the enrollments at Dance Theatre Seattle (which became the Bill Evans Dance Company School) multiplied. By the summer of 1977, we hosted our first six-week Bill Evans Seattle Summer Institute of Dance, which was attended by more than 300 students from all over North America. Our company studios were located in an old neighborhood movie house on Seattle's Capital Hill. Part of the company would remain in Seattle to teach in the flourishing school, and the rest of us would travel under the Dance Touring and Artist in the Schools programs of the National Endowment for the Arts. For a few years, we were the most-booked dance company in the United States, with as many as 40 weeks of touring in a single year. The second of these photographs captures a moment from *The Ashtabula Rag*, named after the small city in northeastern Ohio where we premiered my work about the neurotic behaviors that emerge in dancers who tour for such extended periods.

Peggy Hackney, Gregg Lizenbery, Shirley Jenkins and Regina DeCosse in performance of *The Ashtabula Rag.*
Photograph by David Gotwald (1978)

Jim Coleman, Gregg Lizenbery and Erik Whitmyre in *For Betty*, Meany Hall, Seattle. Photograph by David Gotwald (1979)

Shirley Jenkins, Erik Whitmyre, Debbie Poulsen and Gregg Lizenbery in *Tin-Tal*, Theatre of the Riverside Church, New York City. Photograph by Martha Swope (1979)

Because we were so completely booked so quickly, there was very little time for making new works during the early Seattle years. Much of our repertory, therefore, consisted of the pieces I had choreographed originally for RDT. This version of *For Betty* was part of a children's show we did at the University of Washington's state of the art dance theatre, Meany Hall. This shot of *Tin-Tal* was taken during one of several engagements we completed as part of the Riverside Dance Festival in New York City.

Peggy Hackney, Shirley Jenkins,
Bill Evans, Debbie Poulsen and
Jim Colemen, 1978.

The Legacy was often the centerpiece of concerts given by the Bill Evans Dance Company (BEDCO) around the continent. To a string quartet by Harold Shapero, this 23-minute-long ballet depicts an episode in the life of a polygamous Mormon family in Utah during the late 1800s. It is based on the lives of my great-great-grandfather Abel Evans, his three wives, and his oldest son, as I imagined them.

Evans and Jenkins, 1979.

Evans and Poulsen, foreground,
Hackney and Jenkins,
background.
Photographs of *The Legacy* taken
by David Gotwald (1978)

Hard Times leaves a lot of room for the unique personalities of individual performers to emerge. I particularly enjoyed performing this 20-minute suite of dances with Shirley Jenkins and Erik Whitmyre, who were emotionally and physically raw, vulnerable and fearless. This caused audiences to audibly gasp at several points in their duet.

Bill Evans, Shirley Jenkins and Erik Whitmyre in *Hard Times*.

Photographs by David Gotwald (1979)

Five Songs in August; **Jenkins, Peggy Hackney, Evans, Lizenbery, Jim Coleman and DeCosse.** Photograph by David Gotwald (1978)

The movement vocabulary I had explored and developed over a period of several years crystallized in *Five Songs in August*. In this suite of dances that are both physically demanding and expressively challenging, each dancer is required to activate a large spatial and dynamic range. I last performed the *First Song* in February 2004, during the Bill Evans Dance Company's 30th Anniversary season in Albuquerque, Taos, and Santa Fe, New Mexico. At age 63, I no longer had access to the physical range I had possessed in 1974. I was gratified, however, to discover that my expressive range was even more fully available.

Five Songs in August; **Shirley Jenkins, Bill Evans, Regina DeCosse and Gregg Lizenbery.**

Photograph by David Gotwald (1978)

Jukebox, **Daphne Lowell and Erik Whitmyre in "Jitterbug."**
Photograph by David Gotwald (1978)

Jukebox, **Shirley Jenkins and Bill Evans in "Fred and Ginger."**
Photograph by David Gotwald (1978)

I have had the pleasure of restaging *Jukebox* on numerous casts over the years. This is another of my works in which the unique personalities of the performers must shine through for the choreography to come fully alive. On this page, you see *Little Brown Jug,* first performed by Kathleen McClintock and Gregg Lizenbery, and *Our Love Affair*, which I choreographed for Kay Clark and me.

ON THE AIR

Gregg Lizenbery, Steve
MacArthur, Jim Coleman and
Regina DeCosse in *Jukebox*.
Photograph by
David Gotwald (1978)

My favorite of the six dances in the original *Jukebox* (it has since been extended) is *Take the "A" Train*, based on my memories of Paula Kelly and the Modernaires, who had performed with Glenn Miller and His Orchestra, and whom I saw perform on the Bob Crosby (Bing's younger brother) television program in the early 1950s. Three of the dancers in this photograph are now dance department administrators in higher education: Gregg Lizenbery at the University of Hawaii, Jim Coleman at Mount Holyoke College, and Regina DeCosse at Cabrillo College in Aptos, California. Steve MacArthur has left dance and has become a businessman in New York City.

In the fall of 1977, my company finally had a chance to stay at home in Seattle for several weeks to create a new piece under a generous grant I received from the National Endowment for the Arts. The result was one of the most daring and original works I ever made. For years I had been tormented by a recurring dream—based on numerous real-life experiences—in which I was a boy being mercilessly taunted by other children for my effeminacy. As soon as I started work on this piece, the dreams stopped, and they have never returned. This piece has overt sexuality that offended some of our audiences during cross-country tours in 1977 and 1978. In Salt Lake City the content of this piece made much of the audience extremely uncomfortable, and at least half of the 1,200 people in attendance left the theatre at intermission. For that practical reason, I reluctantly retired this piece after only one year. I have since revived it on two occasions—for a concert called *For Mature Audiences Only* in 2000 and for my company's 28th anniversary reunion in 2002. In the original cast, I played the Boy (alternating with Erik Whitmyre), and Jim Coleman, Regina DeCosse, Peggy Hackney, Shirley Jenkins and Gregg Lizenberg played the taunting children.

Barefoot Boy with Marbles in His Toes.
Photographs by David Gotwald (1977)

In 1978, I purchased an old oyster farm—15 acres of old-growth forest and 500 feet of Hood Canal beachfront—on a very remote point of the Toandos Peninsula in western Washington. I became intoxicated by the serenity and beauty of this magical place. Everything about it was almost completely different from the high Great Basin desert where I had grown up, and I felt as though I was discovering the world all over again. My friend David Sannella, who was then the musical director for the Bill Evans Dance Company and School, had grown up in Arizona. He purchased a houseboat on Seattle's Lake Union, where

Debbie Poulsen, Bill Evans,
Gregg Lizenbery and
Shirley Jenkins in
Impressions of Willow Bay.
Photographs by
Martha Swope (1978)

he also explored the wonderful new watery environment. Together, we agreed to try to capture our impressions of our adopted home. David did so in a score for a chamber orchestra and I did so in a modern dance quartet for members of my company. We created our pieces separately and did not put them together until we both felt that we had completed our individual tasks. The resulting work, *Impressions of Willow Bay*, is one that pleased us both immensely. It received its first formal performances at Seattle's Paramount Theatre in 1978. Roles were shared by: Bill Evans/Erik Whitmyre, Shirley Jenkins/Regina DeCosse/Peggy Hackney, Debbie Poulsen/Daphne Lowell and Gregg Lizenbery/Jim Coleman.

In *Impressions of Willow Bay*, I explored a new way of working. That is, I tried to capture a series of images evoking the life of the natural world on Washington's Olympic Peninsula, as succinctly as possible. Most of my work up to that time had been very metric and rhythmic, with lots of "steps." In *Willow Bay*, I tried to avoid steps and meter, and to find "organic" movement performed by each dancer in personal breath rhythms. The piece, therefore, is exceedingly fragile and can only be performed successfully by an ensemble who are deeply in-tune with one another. The musical score, similarly, creates sound environments rather than stressing meter, rhythm or melody. *Willow Bay* is the kind of subtle and integrated work that can only emerge from collaboration among artists who know one another thoroughly and are willing to let the piece take on its own life in each performance.

Debbie Poulsen, Shirley Jenkins, Gregg Lizenbery and Bill Evans in *Impressions of Willow Bay*, Theatre of the Riverside Church, New York City.
Photograph by Martha Swope (1979)

Impressions of Willow Bay was given a preview showing in an informal setting at the Arcosanti Arts Festival in Arizona. Arcosanti is an experimental "city of the future" founded by Paolo Solari, who invited us to appear there. On this page, you see Debbie Pouslen and me in a moment from *Willow Bay* and Gregg Lizenbery, Shirley Jenkins and me in the final section of *Hard Times*.

Over a number of years, I found myself performing in the same city as Bill Evans the renowned jazz pianist. Many times people came to a theatre where I was giving my solo performance, which I called "Bill Evans in Concert," expecting to hear an evening of jazz music. In 1977 I invited the more famous Bill Evans to dinner during an engagement he was playing at Parnelli's jazz club in Seattle. We decided to try collaborating on a work we would call *Double Bill*. I selected recordings of several of Bill's own compositions, including *Peace Piece, Waltz for Debby* and *The Two Lonely People*, and choreographed a 45-minute collage of set dances and improvisational structures. A few days before our opening, Bill arrived in

Debbie Poulsen and Bill Evans in *Impressions of Willow Bay.* Photograph by David Gotwald (1978)

Shirley Jenkins, Gregg Lizenbery and Bill Evans in *Hard Times.* Photograph by David Gotwald (1978)

Seattle with his sidemen Philly Jo Jones and Mike Moore. The work came together almost magically because the three jazz artists were amazingly aware of, and responsive to, every breath and foot sound we made. Without looking at each other, the BEDCO dancers and the Bill Evans Trio musicians communicated vibrantly. This concert attracted both modern dance and jazz music audiences, and we were sold out almost immediately. The excitement in the theatre was electric, and we received extended standing ovations and ecstatic reviews.

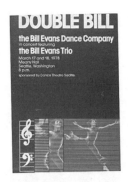

BEDCO Program

Daphne Lowell, Regina DeCosse, Shirley Jenkins, Jim Coleman, Gregg Lizenbery and Bill Evans in *Double Bill*. Photographs by David Gotwald (1978)

Bill Evans in *Double Bill*. Photograph by Marjorie Aronson (1978)

Bill Evans, Debbie Poulsen, Eric Whitmyre, Shirley Jenkins and Gregg Lizenbery in *Double Bill*. Photograph by Martha Swope (1979)

This photograph shows a moment in my opening solo from *Double Bill*. I was 38 and just entering the first stage of my maturity as a performing artist. This image captures the movement qualities I had been trying to capture for many years: dynamic excitement, ease, spatial clarity and spontaneity, embodied within lyricism. Bill and I performed an extended duet at the beginning of our collaborative work before my dancers and his sidemen joined us. I still get goose bumps when I remember the unity I felt with him during those performances. I have had the joy of working with many fine musicians over the ensuing years, but nothing has surpassed my *Double Bill* experience.

Bill Evans gave us permission to perform *Double Bill* to recordings of his music made during our Seattle performances, and we shared this work with cross-country audiences. This photograph shows us (in different costumes) at the Riverside Dance Festival in New York City.

I love performing with and for children, and have done so in K-12 school auditoriums, gymnasiums and cafeterias all over the country, as well as in many formal concerts. The photographs on page 49 show a charming work choreographed by Evans Company member Erik Whitmyre that I have performed with several different children in several different cities since 1979.

In 1979, I collaborated again with Bill Evans. This time, he brought Joe LaBarbera and Mark Johnson as his sidemen. We repeated *Double Bill* and added a second 45-minute piece called *Mixin' It Up*. The first of these pieces is cool, poetic and lyrical; the second is hot, sensual and driving. The highlight of *Mixin' It Up* is a suite of dances I call *Craps* (because it was created in seven-count phrases and requires the dancers to take big risks) performed to an improvisation by Johnson and LaBarbera on bass and drums. On page 50 are four different moments from *Craps*, including dancers Jim Coleman, Debbie Poulsen, Wade Madsen, Rachel Brumer, Gregg Lizenbery, Shirley Jenkins and Sheryl Sedlacek. When Bill Evans died at a tragically young age in 1980, he and I had begun plans for a third collaboration (featuring Latin rhythms) and a tour of Japan.

Bill Evans and Lisette Womak in *Le Miniscule Copain*.

Photographs by David Gotwald (1979)

In 1980, I temporarily modified the name of my company to Bill Evans Dance/Seattle, and Stan Darling created the postcards on page 51 to help us announce the change. To emphasize the addition of "Seattle" to our name, we visited the Boeing Aircraft plant, an international 'Seattle' symbol, for these publicity shots. In the first of these postcards you see numerous tiny images of my leaping body over a large image of the smoldering Mt. St. Helens, another powerful symbol of the Pacific Northwest. In the third of these photographs you see Wade Madsen, Rachel Brumer, Erik Whitmyre, Debbie Poulsen, Bill Evans, Shirley Jenkins, Gregg Lizenbery, Sheryl Sedlacek and Jim Coleman.

Virtually all of our U.S. touring took place under the auspices of the NEA's Dance Touring and/or Artist in the Schools Programs, which required us to be in each location for at least a half-week and

Bill Evans Dance Company in *Craps*.
Photographs by David Gotwald (1979)

often two weeks or more. Therefore, we gave thousands of master classes and hundreds of lecture-demonstrations over our Seattle-based seven years that were devoted primarily to touring. On page 52 you see me teaching a technique master class and a creative movement class, and then conducting a lecture-demonstration during a tour of Indiana, North Carolina, New York, Ohio and Pennsylvania in 1982.

Gregg Lizenbery was my best friend, my dance partner and my life partner from 1967 through 1984. In 1981 and part of 1982, Gregg suffered from a serious back injury and had to stop performing temporarily. To celebrate his return to dancing in October, 1982, we

Publicity/marketing photographs.

Photographs by Stan Darling (1980)

Bill Evans with company member Teri Kraft, Cincinnati, Ohio, 1982. Photograph by unknown

presented a series of Seattle concerts featuring the two of us in two duets, a new solo I made for Gregg and a quartet with company members Debbie Poulsen and Heywood "Woody" McGriff.

During rehearsals for my *Cakewalkin' Babies* in 1982, Gregg Lizenbery, Debbie Poulsen and I posed for *Utah Holiday* magazine.

For our 1983-84 booking brochure, Woody, Gregg, Jeff Bickford and Shannon Loch joined me in capturing a moment from my piece *Diverse Concerto.*

As it turned out, there was no 83-84 BEDCO tour. After a series of farewell concerts at the Playhouse Theatre in Seattle Center in November and December of 1983, the Evans Company closed its Seattle offices and the Bill Evans Dance Company School. I had assumed the position of artistic director of Winnipeg's Contemporary Dancers and its professional conservatory in the summer of 1983 and had been commuting between Winnipeg and Seattle for several months. I loved Seattle more than any other place I had ever lived but

Bill Evans with Teri Kraft, Shannon Loch and Larry Byrne, middle school auditorium, Meadville, Pennsylvania. Photograph by Rick Owens (1982)

Bill Evans with middle school student in Crawfordsville, Pennsylvania.
Photograph by Rick Owens

Gregg Lizenbery and Bill Evans in rehearsal shots from *Alternating Current* **and** *Doin' M' Best.* Photograph by Tom Erlich (1982)

felt compelled to make this change for several reasons. First, the NEA Programs on which my company had depended for touring work— which paid most of the bills and subsidized our self-produced Seattle seasons—were abruptly dismantled under the Reagan administration. Second, as a result, I found myself unable to pay rehearsal salaries to

Bill Evans and Gregg Lizenbery in *Alternating Current.* Photograph by Bill Owens (1985)

Gregg Lizenbery, Debbie Poulsen and Bill Evans in photo for *Utah Holiday* **magazine, which did an issue on prominent Utahans who had left the state.** Photograph by Tom Erlich (1982)

Woody McGriff, Bill Evans, Gregg Lizenbery, Jeff Bickford and Shannon Loch in *Diverse Concerto.* Photograph by Tom Erlich (1983)

my dancers for the first time since our move to Seattle. Third, the Winnipeg Company was awarded more than half a million dollars annually by various federal, provincial and municipal agencies. After working as hard as I could for seven years to make a success of the full-time, professional, Seattle-based Evans organization, I was exhausted and discouraged. I decided to try Canada— where attitudes toward funding the arts are very different from those in the U.S.—in the hopes that I could find a more reasonable life and more time for creative activity.

The Seattle Times, Fall, 1983.

The Collapse, the Search, and then a New Home in New Mexico, 1984–2005

Bill Evans in *Within Bounds*. Photograph by David Gotwald

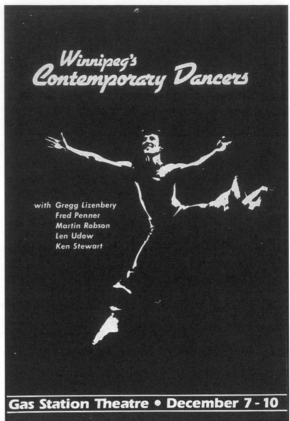

Marketing folder and program for Winnipeg's Contemporary Dancers, 1983–1984.

WINNIPEG'S CONTEMPORARY DANCERS (WCD) WAS ESTABLISHED AT ABOUT THE same time as the Repertory Dance Theatre and is Canada's oldest modern dance company, and one of its most well established. Rachel Browne founded and directed the company for more than 15 years but had been forced into an honorary position by the board of directors. My arrangement with the board was strained from the very beginning. The board president had insisted that our negotiations be kept absolutely secret when he made me a tentative offer to become WCD's artistic director, but then he notified *Maclean's Magazine* and the *Seattle Times* that he had received permission from the Canadian government to make the hire before he even told me. Because I had remained quiet about the tentative offer as requested, my Seattle board and company members were hurt and insulted when they found out about my plans not from me but from the media.

At the end of my first season as artistic director of WCD, we presented an entire concert of my work, called *Dance Art Bill Evans Style*, including a restaging of *Tin-Tal*. At the urging of the board of directors, I invited leading dancers from my Seattle-based company to join WCD. (Debbie Poulsen, shown in the foreground on the left on page 57, had been my student since she was 15.

In 1974, I selected her for the Fairmount Dance Theatre in Cleveland, and in 1976 I invited her to join the Bill Evans Dance Company.) The whole 1983-84 season of four different productions had been a success with Winnipeg critics and audiences, but this season-finale concert was a smash hit.

The highlight of the WCD season-finale concert was the world premiere of my *Prairie Fever*, a 30-minute piece for 10 dancers featuring Gregg Lizenbery, who had accepted the position of permanent guest artist. I was extremely proud of this work, which was the result of several weeks of uninterrupted rehearsal. Responses from Canadian media and funding agencies were overwhelmingly positive. The fact that WCD was handsomely supported by numerous grants meant that it had to earn less that 20 percent of its budget. (My Seattle-based company had earned more than 80 percent of its budget through touring and teaching.)

Karen Unsworth, Debbie Poulsen and Joel Shweky in *Tin-Tal* (left); Unsworth, Shweky, Ruth Cansfield and Chris Gower in *Tin-Tal*. Photographs by Michael Silverwise (1984)

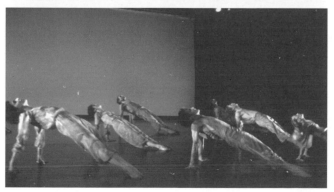

Members of Winnipeg's Contemporary Dancers in *Prairie Fever*. Gregg Lizenbery is the falling figure in the center of the above photograph. Photographs by Michael Silverwise (1984)

Members of Winnipeg's Contemporary Dancers—Karen Unsworth and Chris Gower in *Alternating Current*; Inset: Betty Harless, Joel Shweky, Chris Gower, Karen Unsworth, Bill Evans, David Kurzer and Ruth Cansfield.

Photographs by unknown (1984)

The photographs on page 58 were taken as part of the publicity packet for the 1984-85 WCD Canadian tour—a tour that took place without me. Throughout the spring of 1984 I had been mercilessly harassed by a few Canadian arts activists who objected to the appointment of an American as director of the country's oldest professional modern dance troupe. They were particularly upset that members of my Seattle-based company had joined WCD. Appallingly, the leadership of the WCD board of directors, who made the decision to hire me and then urged me to bring dancers from Seattle, refused to defend or even acknowledge their decisions. In August of 1984, I suffered an acute grief response to the death of my father and the almost simultaneous collapse of my 17-year relationship with Gregg Lizenbery. For just a few days, I suffered a severe emotional collapse. My personal grief made me temporarily unable to withstand the painful public attacks, and I resigned abruptly. In fact this was a call for help. If someone from the board or company had reached out to me, I would have reconsidered my resignation immediately, but I felt so completely alone and abused that I was unable to understand that I really wanted to stay. After less than a week I recovered enough to reconsider my hasty, emotionally-based action, but by then, the president of the board had already named my successor. Because this happened without due process, I might have won a legal battle to regain my position. Deciding that it wasn't worth the expense and aggravation of such a fight, I accepted an offer to remain as resident teacher and choreographer and did what I could to help the new director, Tedd Robinson, avoid the pitfalls I had encountered.

In the spring of 1985, feeling alone and lost, and not knowing what else to do, I returned to Emigration Canyon, near Salt Lake City (where I had designed and supervised the construction of a house in 1974). I found work for a few months as company teacher and choreographer for RDT and guest artist in the University of Utah Department of Modern Dance. This gave me time to spend with my daughter, Tandi, my son-in-law, Troy Densley, and my granddaughter, Ambria, shown in these three photographs. My family helped to fill the enormous void left by the collapse of my Seattle and Winnipeg companies, my break-up with Gregg Lizenbery and the death of my father, and little by little I regained my emotional health and self-confidence.

Top: Bill with Ambria Densley, Port Townsend, Washington, 1982; Middle: Bill and Ambria in solo concert curtain call, Salt Lake City, 1985; Bottom: Bill and Ambria at the Salt Lake City Airport, 1986. Photographs by Gregg Lizenbery, John Brandon and Troy Densley, respectively

Poster for regional American
College Dance Festival, 1987.

From September 1986 through June of 1988, I served as associate professor and coordinator of Modern Dance in the School of Health, Physical Education and Recreation at Indiana University (IU) in Bloomington. I was invited to apply for this position by Fran Syngg, who had coordinated an IU residency by BEDCO in 1982. I worked tirelessly to build the IU Modern Dance Program in every way possible, enjoying considerable success. Pioneer educator Jane Fox, who still lived in Bloomington, and to whom I dedicated the regional American College Dance Festival we hosted in January 1987, had founded this Program. Other faculty members included Gwenn Hamm, Michael Lucas and Debra Knapp, who has been my close friend and professional colleague ever since.

Phase II was a months-long collaboration with remarkably gifted and generous faculty members from other departments: jazz musician David Baker, lighting designer Robert Shakespeare and scenic designer David Higgins. David Baker composed 18 new pieces of music for this production, played live by the IU Jazz Orchestra, which he directed.

Indiana University Dance Theatre in Bill Evans'
Phase II, I.U. Memorial Auditorium.
Photographs by Indiana University News Service (1988)

Bill Evans with dance students
and faculty at the University of
Hawaii at Manoa. Don Halquist
is on the left, front row; dance
instructors Peggy Gaither
and Phyllis Haskell are in the
second row.

Photograph by unknown (1986)

In August 1985, I established a life partnership with Don Halquist, seen in this photograph taken at the University of Hawaii, where I had just choreographed a work called *Tide Pool*, in the spring of 1986. Don was a graphic designer who wanted to become a dancer. He first studied with me in November of 1984, during a residency I completed at Allegheny College. In 1985, he enrolled in my summer institutes in Meadville, Pennsylvania and Port Townsend, Washington. Neither of us thought that a long-term relationship was possible, because of our 21-year age difference. After a few months, however, we both realized that for us chronological age is just a number and that what we had in common was too powerful to ignore. We celebrated our 20th anniversary on August 4, of 2005.

Both Don and I loved Indiana University and Bloomington. Nonetheless, feeling a powerful pull from the ancient cultures of the "Land of Enchantment," I accepted an invitation to become head of dance at the University of New Mexico (UNM) in August of 1989. These photographs show two views of the old adobe hacienda that we rehabilitated in the village of Corrales, northwest of Albuquerque. The first is of Don and me with our dog Sushi (who died in 2003 at age 16 ½) in the living room. The second shows an entrance to the portal.

Sushi, Don Halquist and Bill Evans.
Photograph by Roz Schrodt

**Entering the portal of the Evans-Halquist home in
Corrales, New Mexico.** Photograph by Bill Evans (1992)

Don Halquist, Virginia Nicholas, Debra Landau, Licia Perea and Eva Encinias-Sandoval in Bill Evans' *Craps*. Photographs by John Malolepsy (1988)

These photographs show two moments in my work *Craps*, which I restaged for the University of New Mexico Dance Program's fall concert in 1988. All of these dancers appeared with the Albuquerque-based Bill Evans Dance Company over a period of several years. Don Halquist is now an assistant professor of education and human development at the State University of New York College at Brockport, as well as a part-time professional dancer and dance teacher. Virginia Nicholas directs her own Pilates/yoga studio in Tempe, Arizona. Debra Landau directs her own modern dance company and performance space in Albuquerque. Licia Perea has a successful solo concert career and Pilates practice based in Los Angeles. Eva Encinias-Sandoval is a full professor of dance at UNM and artistic director of an internationally known flamenco festival.

Bill Evans with students in the UNM Dance Program. Photograph by Pat Berrett (1992)

Ambria Densley and Bill Evans in the Sandia Mountains east of Albuquerque. Photograph by Albert Noyer (1994)

I have loved teaching since my first professional teaching job at the Irene J. Earl School of Dance in American Fork, Utah, when I was 13 years old. Since I stepped down from the head of dance position at UNM in 1992, however, I have focused on teaching as my primary activity, and it has gradually become the most important component of my life. Here I am with a group of UNM dance majors after a modern dance technique class. The second image is of me with my granddaughter Ambria, who studied dance in the Salt Lake Valley in Utah for more than 15 years. In this shot, we are visiting the Sandia Mountain home of my friends Albert and Jennifer Noyer during one of my annual summer institutes of dance in Albuquerque. Ambria had come from her home in Herriman, Utah to study with me.

Members of the UNM Contemporary Dance Ensemble in Bill Evans' *Danza.*

Photographs by John Malolepsy (1992)

In 1989, I founded the UNM Contemporary Dance Ensemble. For the next several years, this group of undergraduate and graduate student dance majors performed in schools and senior centers throughout New Mexico and in UNM's Rodey Theatre, the primary performance venue for the Department of Theatre and Dance. This page shows two moments from one of three works I choreographed for the troupe in 1992, *Danza*, to music by Inti-Illimani. My other two works were *Bob's Blues*, a suite of rhythm tap dances, and *Jumpin' With Jefferson*, a jazz work. Both were performed with the namesake composers/performers on stage. Bob Tate is a pianist and Jefferson Vorhees is a drummer. Both were then accompanying classes in the UNM Dance Program.

Left: Bill Evans and Virginia Wilmerding in *Jukebox* (1989). Photograph by John Malolepsy. Right: Sara Hutchinson and Bill Evans in *Blues Suite*. Photograph by Pat Berrett (1990)

In my first year at UNM, I established performing and teaching relationships that lasted until my departure from New Mexico in July 2004. Both Ginny Wilmerding and Sara Hutchinson served as adjunct faculty in the UNM Dance Program, and both performed with me many times in university performances and in BEDCO Concerts.

In 1992, I choreographed and produced my first entire evening of (mostly) tap dance, which I called *The Festival of Percussive Dance*. This concert was performed to live music by the Jack Manno Jazz Ensemble and included not only tap dances but also fusions of tap with flamenco, tap with Irish step dancing and tap with Appalachian clogging. The nucleus of performers assembled for this project continued to work with me for the next decade, and became known as the Bill Evans Rhythm Tap Ensemble (BERTE).

Left: Jolene Ray, Misty Owens, Joel Carino, Sara Hutchinson and Skip Randall in *Festival of Percussive* Dance; Right: Bill Evans Rhythm Tap Ensemble (Evans on floor) in *Be Seated*. Photographs by John Malolepsy (1992)

In 1991, as a community service, I founded the Albuquerque Youth Dance Troupe. Dancers between the ages of eight and 18 were selected in open auditions. For several years, I choreographed original works for this children's company for the annual Dance Magnifico concert, part of the City of Albuquerque's annual festival of the arts. On this page, you see a moment from *Espiritus de la Tierra* and its curtain call. I made this piece in collaboration with Santa Fe sculptor/fabric artist Edwin Rivera, who directed other children in creating huge sculptures that became integral parts of the dance work.

Albuquerque Youth Dance Troupe in Bill Evans' *Espiritus de la Tierra.* **Photographs by Pat Berrett (1992)**

Publicity flyer for the Bill Evans Dance Company on tour, early 1990's.

In the early and middle 1990s, the Albuquerque-based Bill Evans Dance Company started once again to tour nationally and internationally, as much as my position as a professor of dance at UNM would allow. This is the flyer we sent to sponsors to help them market our performances, master classes and workshops. Herbert Migdoll took the photograph of me performing my "Tennis" solo from *Jukebox* during a performance at Dance Theatre Workshop in New York City.

For several years, the performances of the Bill Evans Rhythm Tap Ensemble and Bill Evans Dance Company were accompanied by live music, under the direction of Jack Manno. The first of the photographs on page 67 is a publicity shot we sent to sponsors. The second captures the final moment of the "Modernaires" section of *Jukebox*, part of an evening of jazz-flavored contemporary dance and rhythm tap dance called *Fascinatin' Rhythms*, which we performed at colleges and universities in several states.

Left: Jack Manno, Skip Randall, Sara Hutchinson, Bill Evans and Rick Fairbanks, publicity photograph for the Bill Evans Rhythm Tap Ensemble; Right: Don Halquist, Skip Randall, Linda Johnson-Gallegos and Billbob Brown in *Jukebox.* Photographs by Pat Berrett (1993)

My work at UNM was the subject of a cover story in the May/June, 1993 issue of *Dance Teacher Now* magazine. Writer Liz Fruits is the daughter of Taos, New Mexico dance pioneer Bette Winslow and the aunt of a former UNM dance major and BEDCO company member, Adrienne Ponds.

In 1993, Japanese dance educators and businessmen hosted the first (and only) International College Dance Festival. I was selected by the board of directors of the (American) National Dance Association to take the UNM Contemporary Dance Ensemble to Kobe, Japan as the only representatives of the United States to participate in this prestigious event. The festival organizers paid all of our expenses and treated us royally. In addition to our appearances at the College Festival, I organized performances at the Mukogawa Women's University and the American Festival in Sasebo, an Albuquerque Sister City. This photograph shows me with the mayor of Sasebo (far right), two prominent Sasebo business leaders (far left), Gwen Owens (mother of Misty Owens—one of the dancers), Sidney Ortiz and Adrienne Clancy (undergraduate and graduate UNM dance majors). Our Japanese hosts were warm and gracious, and I still cherish lovely memories of that three-week visit. At the end of this tour I went to Tokyo, where I performed solo works as the representative of American professional dance at the Japanese Asian Dance Event, a weeklong festival for artists from Pacific Rim countries.

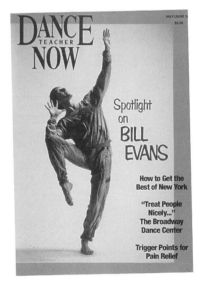

Cover of *Dance Teacher Now* **magazine, May/June, 1993.**

Bill Evans and others at a reception given by the mayor of Sasebo, Japan.

Photograph by Suzanne Ryan (1993)

In December of 1993 and January of 1994, I taught and performed in several locations in the states of Maharashtra and Karnataka, India, at the invitation of Prabha Marate, director of the Kala Chhaya Cultural Institute in Pune. These photographs show me in ancient caves at Ellora, near Arangabad, Maharashtra, and with students at the Ninasam Theatre Institute in Heggodu, Karnataka. I choreographed a solo for myself in response to my life-changing experiences on this tour, *How To Name It,* to music by the Indian composer Ilaiyaraaja. I revived that piece in April 2005 for appearances with the Chicago Tap Theatre and its production called *The Legacy of Bill Evans: Master of Movement*, which honored me as I approached age 65.

From 1991 through 2001, I made several tours of Mexico, some with my company, some as a soloist and one with the UNM Contemporary Dance

Ensemble. The proximity of New Mexico to "old" Mexico made such tours both relevant and feasible. I learned to speak Spanish and grew to know and love Mexican culture. My home is now full of colorful Mexican folk art that delights me daily. BEDCO performed in Guanajuato at the Teatro Juarez, shown in this photograph, in 1994. It is splendidly ornate and majestic, in the Spanish colonial style. It presented us with the challenge of a steeply raked stage, something I hadn't encountered in the U.S. since my tour with Ruth Page in 1966.

Bill Evans in front of the Teatro Juarez, Guanajuato, Mexico.

Photograph by Rip Parker (1994)

In 1997, the Bill Evans Dance Company and the Evans Rhythm Tap Ensemble presented a concert called *Albuquerque Love Song* (also the title of my new solo to music by Michael Cava) on Valentine's Day weekend, at UNM's Rodey Theatre. Shown on this page are: a) Don Halquist and Linda Johnson-Gallegos in *Tango*; b) Don Halquist, Linda Johnson-Gallegos and I in *Tin-Tal*; c) Sara Hutchinson, Skip Randall and I in *Be Seated*; and d) Hutchinson, Randall, Mark Yonally and I in the collaboratively-choreographed *Los Ritmos Calientes*.

In 1997, I was selected as the National Dance Association (NDA) Scholar/Artist. I had been active in NDA in various capacities since 1977, when my professional company performed at the Heritage Award ceremony for Elizabeth R. (Betty) Hayes in Seattle. From 1993 through 1996 I served as NDA Vice President for Performance. On the next page, you see the cover of NDA's *Spotlight on Dance*, announcing my selection as Scholar/Artist and my friend Kathy Kinderfather's selection as the 1997 Heritage Honoree. Also shown is a photograph of me receiving the Scholar/Artist Award from NDA president Lynnette Overby in St. Louis. My Scholar/Artist lecture was illustrated by BEDCO dancers Don Halquist and Debra Landau and culminated with my performance of *Albuquerque Love Song*.

BEDCO/BERTE in *Albuquerque Love Song*, **February 1997.**

Photographs by Pat Berrett

Left: Cover of the National
Dance Association's *Spotlight on
Dance*, winter, 1997;
Right: Bill Evans and Lynnette
Overby, March, 1997.
Photograph by Thais Evans

My lecture, *Teaching What I Want to Learn*, has been published as a booklet by NDA/AAHPERD Publications and—in a modified version—as an article in the journal *Contact Quarterly*, Summer/Fall, 1999. (The lecture is included as Appendix III.)

In June 1997, Don Halquist and I sold our old adobe hacienda in the historic village of Corrales, northwest of Albuquerque, and moved into a new adobe hacienda on more than 12 acres in the Sandia Mountains, northeast of Albuquerque. These photographs show the view from the kitchen to the great room and the back portal and deck in the summer of 1998. The mountain house is constructed in the traditional Pueblo style, with brick and Mexican saltillo tile floors and cottonwood *vigas* and *latillas*. The house was both our home and the headquarters of the Bill Evans Dance Company and the New Mexico Contemporary Dance Alliance, with a studio, offices, video library, costume storage rooms and a *casita* for visiting artists. The majestic beauty of the New Mexican high desert was everywhere—offering serene quiet, star-filled skies and thrilling sunrises.

Evans/Halquist home in the New Mexico mountains, 1997–2004.

Photographs by Bill Evans

In 1997, the Regional Dance America (RDA) organization produced the first ever National Ballet Festival, in Houston, Texas, with performances by more than 100 companies from across the country. I was honored to be one of five adjudicators/artistic directors for this landmark event. The first photograph on page 71 appeared in *Dance Teacher Now* magazine and shows the five artistic directors dressed for a rodeo, one of the bonus features of this several-day festival. I have been honored many times since 1982 with invitations to act as an adjudicator for the American College Dance Festival Association, RDA and several regional organizations. I cherish such opportunities to share my perceptions, encourage young artists and act as an advocate for dance in our culture.

In January of 1999, BEDCO staged the first of several 25th anniversary productions, at Albuquerque's South Broadway Cultural Center. This archival photograph

Left: Robert Barnett, Maria Grandy, Bill Evans, Sally Brayley Bliss and Jeffrey Gribler, 1997. Photograph by Don Halquist:

Right: Poster design by Don Halquist; photograph by Martha Swope: *Silver*, January 1999.

Above: Skip Randall and Bill Evans in *Silver Tones*;
Left: Sara Hutchinson, Mark Yonally, Randall and Evans in the same work.
Photographs by Pat Berrett (1999)

shows Shirley Jenkins, Bill Evans, Erik Whitmyre and Debbie Poulsen, members of the original cast of *Impressions of Willow Bay*, a 1978 work revived for the occasion. In the anniversary gala, *Silver*, it was performed by Don Halquist, Denise Herrera, Linda Johnson-Gallegos and Rip Parker.

The other photographs are from Act II of *Silver*, a suite of rhythm tap dances performed by Hovey Corbin, Bill Evans, Sara Hutchinson, Brenna Kuhn, Skip Randall and Mark Yonally.

For BEDCO's 25th anniversary season, we performed several different concerts throughout New Mexico with support from the New Mexico Arts

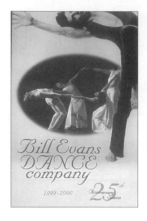

Poster for *First Annual New Mexico Tap Dance Jam* and *End of the Trail.* Photographs by Pat Berrett (summer, 1999).

Cover for BEDCO 1999 - 2000 season touring program; photographs by Pat Berrett (Halquist, Johnson-Gallegos, Herrera and Parker in *Impressions of Willow Bay*) and Jack Mitchell (Evans in *Five Songs in August*).

Division and the National Endowment for the Arts. We gave numerous concerts in Albuquerque and touring performances in Santa Fe, Taos, Sandia Park, Placitas, Los Alamos and Soccorro.

In June of 1999, I produced the first *New Mexico Tap Dance Jam*, a community tap celebration featuring the Evans Rhythm Tap Ensemble and national guest artists and including dancers of many ages from several private studios. In August of 1999, my company performed *End of the Trail*, a tribute to Bella Lewitzky, which featured a revival of her masterwork *Ceremony*, staged by former Lewitzky company dancer Walter Kennedy and Bella's daughter, Nora Reynolds Daniel.

I produced my first evening of percussive dance in 1992, and I have presented numerous evenings of tap dance on many occasions since then in several U.S. states, in Monterrey, Mexico, and in Kuopio, Finland. In 1999, however, I increased the amount of my time and creative energy devoted to tap dance when I directed and produced the first annual New Mexico Tap Dance Jam. The Jam has since become a traditional community celebration of this art form in both Santa Fe and Albuquerque. (The seventh annual jam—for which I served as guest artist/director—took place in May of 2005, in both Santa Fe and Albuquerque.)

End of the Trail is the title of a work performed extensively by the Evans Dance Company in the middle and late 1970s. It is one of several works I revived for a concert with the same title in which we honored Bella Lewitzky. Bella had moved to Albuquerque after closing her own illustrious company in Los Angeles. She honored us as well, by allowing BEDCO to be the first company other than her own to perform one of her pieces.

I have taught intensive summer dance programs since 1970, but in June of 1999 I produced and directed my first summer program exclusively for professional dance teachers, at the University of New Mexico in Albuquerque.

BEDCO in *End of the Trail*; **Left: Don Halquist; Right: Jessica Jahner, Don Halquist, Erin Clotworthy and Rebecca Blackwell-Hafner.**
Photographs by Pat Berrett (1999)

The Bill Evans Rhythm Tap Ensemble in rehearsal for and after a performance of the first annual *New Mexico Tap Dance Jam*; **Left: Misty Owens, Mark Yonally, Wendy Leverenz Barker, Bruce Stegmann (guest artist), Jeannie Hill (guest artist) and Skip Randall; Right: Diane Gutierrez, Brian Molina, Warrena Padilla, Sara Hutchinson, Randall, Owens, Hill, Barker, Yonally and Brenna Kuhn.** Photographs by Bill Evans (1999)

(Facing the camera) Don Halquist, Kristin Carpenter, Bill Evans, Kitty Daniels, Sarah Manglesdorf, Joan Gonwa and Helen Myers, participants in the first annual Evans Dance Teachers' Intensive, June, 1999.
Photograph by Kathy Moore

Since then, such programs have been conducted many times, in such locations as Port Townsend, Washington, Indianapolis, Indiana, Brockport, New York, Nanaimo, British Columbia and Puebla, Mexico. Faculty have included: Kitty Daniels, Don Halquist, Debra Knapp, Suzie Lundgren, Rip Parker, Kista Tucker and Suzanne Oliver.

In 2000, *Dance Teacher* and *Dance Spirit* magazines published articles about my teaching with photographs by Santa Fe photographer James Black.

Cover of *Dance Teacher* magazine, January, 2000, and article in *Dance Spirit* magazine, April, 2000, photographs of Bill Evans by James Black.

the dancer's body

By Mark Yonally

Mark is a member of the Bill Evans Dance Company and will be working with Bruce Stegmann's ETC, a rhythm tap company based in Chicago. Mark recently served as a faculty member at Oklahoma City University.

In Attitude

Dance master Bill Evans on listening to YOUR body.

As Bill Evans prepares for a solo concert in honor of his 60th birthday (April 11), the depth and intelligence he applies to his dancing not only garners international attention, but also allows him to dance nearly injury-free. But the expert dancer/choreographer/teacher who founded and directs the Bill Evans Dance Company, a solo repertory and summer dance institute, says it wasn't always that way.

Physical challenges multiplied as Bill's career progressed, dancing with companies including Utah Civic Ballet (now Ballet West), Ruth Page Chicago Ballet, Lyric Opera Of Chicago, Louisville Civic Ballet, Washington Ballet, Atlanta Ballet and Repertory Dance Theatre Of Utah. In 1969, after years of training in ballet, modern and jazz, Bill discovered

chronic injuries that threatened the longevity of his career. The man who has been devoted to dance since age 3, holding marbles between his toes so he could tap like Gene Kelly and Fred Astaire, says, "I just wasn't willing to continue dancing in a way that was injuring my body and would force me to retire after a few more years." Today, with performances, choreographic works and accolades numbering in the thousands, Bill no longer plays with marbles, but still has the same enthusiasm he had when he started training back in 1948.

"In the '50s and '60s, most dance teachers didn't have the opportunity to study anatomy and kinesiology. We often danced on non-resilient floors (such as tile over concrete) and were not encouraged to stop dancing when injured, but were praised for trying to ignore pain and to 'work through our injuries,'" Bill explains. He took the matter into his own hands. "I had to learn to accept the realities of my physical structure and to like my body for what it was rather than hate it for what it was not. I started paying more attention to what was happening inside. I discovered that

This portrait by James Black is my mother's favorite image of me. Mom—Lila Evans—turned 92 on November 2, 2004.

In January 2001, New Mexico free-lance choreographers Celia Dale, Lane Lucas, Jill Pribyl and Helen Myers joined me in a Santa Fe/Albuquerque production called *For Mature Audiences Only*. At a time when audiences for modern dance were generally shrinking, this concert received extraordinary amounts of publicity and all performances were sold out in advance. For this occasion, I revived two older works and created two new ones, including *Stand By Your Man* for Don Halquist and me.

In 2001, I received the New Mexico Governor's Award for Excellence and Achievement in the Arts—the third dancer ever to be so honored. The photograph on page 76 shows me with Dee and Gary

Photograph by James Black, November 1999.

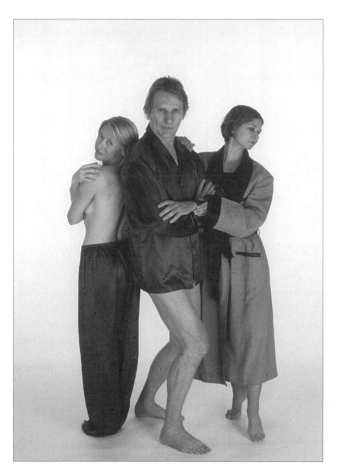

For Mature Audiences Only (January 2001); Left: Lane Lucas, Bill Evans and Jill Pribyl in publicity shot; Right: Don Halquist and Bill Evans in *Stand By Your Man*. Photographs by Pat Berrett

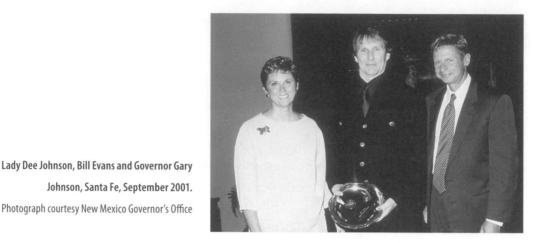

First Lady Dee Johnson, Bill Evans and Governor Gary Johnson, Santa Fe, September 2001.
Photograph courtesy New Mexico Governor's Office

Johnson at the historic Palace of the Governors in Santa Fe, where the ceremony was held. In my acceptance speech I made a plea for more movement and dance programs in New Mexico schools. (It is included as an appendix to this book.)

For the 2001–2002 main-stage season of the UNM Department of Theatre and Dance, my Dance Program faculty colleagues honored me by giving me the unprecedented opportunity (for one faculty member) to present an entire evening of work. I choreographed and restaged works for the UNM Dance Company, for members of the UNM Dance Program faculty and for my professional Bill Evans Dance Company. I called the evening *Reflections and Beginnings*. Seen here are moments from my works *Remembering* and *Fusion*, the latter of which I co-choreographed with world-renowned flamenco artist Eva Encinias-Sandoval. This cast of *Remembering* was selected for the gala performance at the American College Dance Festival at Arizona State University a few weeks later. The entire concert received the Bravo Award for Excellence in Dance from the Albuquerque Arts Alliance—the second time I received that honor.

Reflections and Beginning (February, 2002); Left: Malu Pelaez, Jessica Searer, Aline Casanova, Cristiane Oliviera, Kelly Ferguson, Elizabeth Marie Nevada and Sara Yanney in *Remembering*; Right: Eva Encinias-Sandoval and Bill Evans in *Fusion*.
Photographs by John Malolepsy

For *Reflections and Beginnings*, I revived my Mormon family drama, *The Legacy*, with a new version of the set designed for the very first version of this work in 1972. Sadly, those February and March 2002, performances of my role in this piece were my last, at age 61. Because the role requires extensive lifting of all three of my "wives" and of my adult "son," I have not attempted the role since. My injury-free body and ability to dance fully depends on working carefully with my body's evolving realities. At this point, such extensive lifting would not be wise. It is a role I performed over 30 years with numerous casts of "wives" and "sons."

As in dozens of other creative projects since 1988, I collaborated with lighting designer John Malolepsy, professor of design for performance at UNM, on *Reflections and Beginnings*. To thank Professor Malolepsy for his years of artistic excellence, I re-awarded my 2002 Bravo Award to him in the Albuquerque Arts Alliance ceremony of April 2002.

Along with the annual New Mexico Tap Jams, I produced annual New Mexico Rhythm Tap Festivals at UNM. These photographs show me with students in the fourth annual festival, which was supported by grants from the New Mexico Arts Division/National Endowment for the Arts and the City of Albuquerque

The Legacy from Reflections and Beginnings (February 2002); **Left: Don Halquist and Debra Landau; Right: Bill Evans, Debra Landau, Don Halquist and Linda Johnson-Gallegos.**
Photographs by John Malolepsy

Don Halquist, Linda Johnson-Gallegos, Eric Hall and Denise Herrera in *Impressions of Willow Bay* from *Reflections and Beginnings* (February, 2002).
Photograph by John Malolepsy

Bill Evans with students in the fourth annual New Mexico Festival Tap Festival, University of New Mexico, June, 2002.

Photographs by Don Halquist

Urban Enhancement Trust Fund. Tap Festival faculties have included: Bril Barrett, Bill Evans, Acia Gray, Jeannie Hill, Sara Hutchinson, Brenna Kuhn, Jackie Church Oliver, Misty Owens, Skip Randall, Bruce Stegmann, Mark Yonally and Virginia Wilmerding. The national dance community has noticed my intense involvement in rhythm tap, and in the first ever *Dance Magazine* Readers Choice Poll (June, 2004) I was named one of the country's three top tap dancers (along with Savion Glover and Brenda Bufalino).

Many of my former tap students have gone on to successful careers. Mark Yonally, for example, is now artistic director of the Chicago Tap Theatre; Hovey Corbin teaches music and dance at the Albuquerque Academy; Brenna Kuhn is a member of Acia Gray's Tapestry Dance Company in Austin, Texas; Misty Owens is a member of the Peggy Spina Tap Dance Company in New York City; and Sara Hutchinson is dance coordinator for Albuquerque Public Schools.

4th annual New Mexico Tap Dance Jam (May, 2002); Above: front—Hovey Corbin and Brenna Kuhn, back—Mark Yonally, Acia Gray, Skip Randall, Bill Evans, Misty Owens, Sara Hutchinson and Jack Manno; Right: Bill Evans and Brill Barrett.

Photographs by Don Halquist

In the summer of 2002, with grants from the UNM Research Allocations Committee and the Manitoba (Canada) Arts Council, I was able to actualize a project I had dreamed of for several years. Because I am on the permanent guest faculty of Winnipeg's School of Contemporary Dancers, I have had the opportunity to significantly influence the artistic development of many young Canadian professional dancers. For a project called *Summer Love*, I brought Kyla Wallace as an apprentice to my own company, Linnea Swan and Randy Joynt, principal dancers in TRIP Dance Company, and Hugh Conacher, prominent Canadian lighting designer, from Winnipeg to Albuquerque. These Canadian artists joined Don Halquist, Linda Johnson-Gallegos and Elizabeth Marie Nevada of BEDCO in a new work I call *Songs of Ancient Summer.* This is the most personally meaningful work I created during the 16 years in which my company rehearsed and performed at UNM, and a source of great artistic satisfaction.

Kyla Wallace, Elizabeth Marie Nevada, Don Halquist, Linda Johnson-Gallegos, Randy Joynt and Linnea Swan, after rehearsal for *Songs of Ancient Summer*, University of New Mexico, July, 2002. Photograph by Bill Evans

From 1980 through 1985 and again since 2001, I have had the pleasure of teaching and performing each summer for Centrum Arts and Education at Fort Worden State Park, Port Townsend, Washington. Sea, mountains and a charming Victorian village surround this location. It is, for me, the perfect site for intensive creative work.

In August 2002, Centrum hosted the 28th anniversary reunion of the Bill Evans Dance Company between sessions of my annual Dance Teachers' Intensive. I feared that we may not make it to 30 years, and took advantage of a Centrum residency to bring together current and former members and associates

Bill Evans with participants in his annual Dance Teachers' Intensive, Port Townsend, Washington (August 2002); Above: session in Bartenieff Fundamentals—foreground, Kathy Moore, Evans, Robbyn Scott and Jane Stewart; background, Cheryl MacDonald, Cheryl Adams, Cathy Davalos, Joan Gonwa, Kristin Carpenter Torok, Sarah Manglesdorf and Ming L'Hui (in the corner is musician Eric Chappelle); Below: culmination of course in Evans Modern Dance Technique.

Photographs by Keven Elliff, courtesy of Centrum

Bill Evans with participants in the 28th anniversary reunion of the Bill Evans Dance Company, Port Townsend, Washington, August 2002. Photograph by Keven Elliff, courtesy of Centrum

of my professional modern dance company from a 28-year span. Most have gone on to careers as company directors, choreographers, college or university professors, dance department heads, arts managers, filmmakers, fitness specialists or movement therapists. Participants came from several U.S. states, Canada, Mexico and New Zealand.

The final work on the Bill Evans Dance Company 28th Anniversary Reunion Concert was my 1985 solo, *Dances for My Father*, shown on the next page.

The entire cast joined me for a curtain call—the culmination of the Bill Evans Dance Company 28th Anniversary Concert.

In April 2003, Skip Randall—at age 79—gave his final performances as a member of my Rhythm Tap Ensemble. Here he is (on page 82) with the whole group and guest artist Acia Gray, just after his final appearance.

Curtain call of the BEDCO 28th Anniversary Reunion Concert (l – r, Jim Coleman, Zoe Coleman, Terese Freedman, Evan Coleman, Wade Madsen, Don Halquist, Charlene Curtiss, Joanne Petroff, Shirley Jenkins, Bill Evans, Linda Johnson-Gallegos, Jennifer DeLeon, Sidney Anderson, Nancy Van Deusen, Greg Torok, Dan Dalley, Mary Jean Van Almen, Kristin Carpenter Torok, Lynn Schmidt, Colleen Curtis, Christian Swenson, Holly Bright and Gail Heilbron).

Photograph by Keven Elliff, courtesy of Centrum

Bill Evans performs *Dances for My Father* in the 28th anniversary reunion concert of the Bill Evans Dance Company, McCurdy Pavilion, Fort Worden State Park, Port Townsend, Washington, August 11, 2002. Photograph by Keven Elliff, courtesy of Centrum

Front—Mark Yonally, Brenna Kuhn, Acia Gray and Elizabeth Gallea, back—Jackie Church Oliver, Wendy Leverenz Barker, Laura Sicignano, Bill Evans, Skip Randall and Sara Hutchinson, 5th annual *New Mexico Tap Dance Jam*, Outpost Performance Space, Albuquerque, April, 2003. Photograph by Lois Randall

I love teaching dancers of all ages and abilities. Teaching teachers, however, is especially rewarding; they are incredibly supportive, demonstrative and appreciative of the opportunity to receive information, guidance and feedback. Here I am conducting a modern class in my 2003 Dance Teachers' Intensive and performing in the culminating concert, *Dances from Centrum*.

Above: Bill Evans teaching modern dance technique; Left: Evans performing a tap solo in *Dances from Centrum*, Port Townsend, Washington. Photographs by Keven Elliff, courtesy of Centrum (August, 2003)

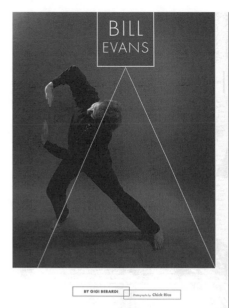

BY GIGI BERARDI   Photographs by Chick Rice

38   DANCE MAGAZINE

Title pages from a feature article in *Dance Magazine*. Photographs of Bill Evans by Chick Rice (October, 2003)

In October 2003, K.C. Patrick, then the editor-in-chief of *Dance Magazine*, fulfilled a long-time intention of publishing a feature article about me. It was called "Bill Evans: Changing the Body and the Geography of Modern Dance" and was written by Gigi Berardi. Vancouver, British Columbia photographer, Chick Rice, visited me during a residency with the Dance Gallery of Bellingham, Washington, to take these portraits in the summer of 2003. (Originally, they were intended for the cover, but were bumped by the art director at the last minute in favor of a photograph of a Russian ballerina.) The article, however, was definitely the highlight of the issue, and I am deeply grateful to K.C. for making it possible.

For *Thirty—the New Mexico Farewell Tour*, the Bill Evans Company presented a concert of old and new works. One of the revivals was *Velorio*, which I choreographed in 1991.

30th Anniversary Performances of the Bill Evans Dance Company, South Broadway Cultural Center, Albuquerque, February, 2004; two moments from *Velorio*; Above: foreground—Kyla Wallace, Elizabeth Marie Nevada and Crystal Fernandez; Below: Wallace and Nevada. Photographs by Pat Berrett

30th Anniversary Performances of the Bill Evans Dance Company, South Broadway Cultural Center, Albuquerque, February, 2004; Above: Don Halquist and Debra Knapp in *Segundo Tango*; Below: Elizabeth Marie Nevada, Bill Evans and Kyla Wallace in *Rhythms of the Earth*. Photographs by Pat Berrett

Another revival for *Thirty* was *Tres Tangos*, performed by Debra Knapp and Don Halquist. The major new work for my company's final New Mexico season was *Rhythms of the Earth*, in which eight tap dancers play a percussion score with their feet and dance with eight modern dancers. The first work in which I integrated dancing by modern and tap ensembles simultaneously was *Together Through Time*, which I choreographed for student dancers at the University of Central Oklahoma in Edmond under a grant from Dance USA's National College Choreography Initiative. I revived and expanded *Together Through Time* for dance majors at the State University of New York (SUNY) College at Brockport in February of 2005.

All good things must come to an end, but it was not easy to say goodbye to something as nourishing to my being as my own dance company. In February, 2004—after thousands of performances, representing tens of thousands of hours of rehearsals and classes and countless other related activities—the Bill Evans Dance Company gave its final curtain calls. My major creative outlets in the future will be the student and professional companies who invite me to create or restage work as a guest artist.

On April 28, 2004, shortly after a New Mexico tour of my annual New Mexico Tap Dance Jam, hundreds of friends and current and former students joined Don Halquist and me in the Carlisle Performance Space at UNM to say farewell. It was an emotionally-charged occasion, and a very gratifying one. On July 1, 2004, I became professor of dance emeritus at UNM. A few weeks later, I began an appointment as a visiting professor/guest artist at the State University of New York College at Brockport.

Wendy Leverenz Barker, Donna Jewell, Debra Knapp, Bill Evans, Don Halquist, Kyla Wallace, Mandy Lamb and Crystal Fernandez enjoy a standing ovation after one of the 30th Anniversary Performances of the Bill Evans Dance Company. Photograph by Pat Berrett

The UNM Department of Theatre and Danc

faculty and staff invite you to a farewell reception for Professor Bill Evans and his partner Don Halquist on:

Wednesday, April 28th
6:00 pm - 8:00 pm
Carlilse Performance Studio
Carlisle Gym
UNM Campus

A performance of Evans' newest work *"Rythms of the Earth"* will be shown from 6:30 pm - 6:45 pm.

Professor Evans will retire from UNM on July 1st after 16 years of service. He will become Artist in Residence in the Department of Dance at the State University of New York at Brockport, where Mr. Halquist will become Assistant Professor of Education in August.

Please drop by to say goodbye.

Bill Evans

Of course, I'll never stop dancing. Since my "retirement," I have:

- given two annual *Bill Evans and Friends Dance Concerts* at Centrum Arts and Education in Port Townsend, Washington;
- performed with Light Motion Dance and Don Halquist at Middlebury College in Vermont;
- danced with 15 students from the SUNY Brockport Dance Department in the annual DANSCORE concert;
- performed as a featured guest with the Chicago Tap Theatre, the 7th Annual New Mexico Tap Dance Jams and the San Diego Tap Festival;
- danced in the first-ever University of Utah Modern Dance Department Alumni Concert;
- given informal lecture-performances at the California State Summer School of the Arts and at the Firehouse Performing Arts Center in Bellingham, Washington; and
- given two solo concerts at SUNY Brockport to celebrate my 65th birthday.

On April 3, 2004, Lucia Mauro, dance critic for the Chicago Tribune, wrote about my appearances with the Chicago Tap Theatre, directed by my former student and company member, Mark Yonally:

> *It's evident that these two artists share a bond of fearless experimentation rooted in laser-precise technique. Most noticeable were the many shades and tones of their taps, including a softness that creates a sophisticated rhythmic language of relaxed virtuosity….His breadth of experience in ballet, modern and tap dance has molded Evans into a uniquely lyrical-percussive artist. And while fusion might be an easy buzzword to slap onto his merging of styles, he more accurately melds each discipline into the other so that only movement—with no titles attached—remains.*

I am humbled and delighted by Ms. Mauro's perceptions and descriptions, but it is not the approval of others that drives me to continue dancing. Remarkably, it is still true at age 65 that I am alive when performing to a degree I rarely experience at other times. I am fully present in body-mind and the moment; I feel vibrant in each cell of my body and every second of time; my senses of hearing and movement are exquisitely intense; breath and body sounds of the audience guide my choices of phrasing and dynamics. I am transported to a wondrously compelling and harmonious world, and the months of stress-producing work— choreographing, rehearsing, scheduling, selecting costumes, designing lights,

Facing page: Poster for University of New Mexico farewell reception for Bill Evans and Don Halquist, April, 2004.

Photograph by Steve Clarke

coordinating with producers, technicians and marketing personnel, watching my diet and staying in shape—seem well spent. I perceive dance as primarily an activity of the human spirit. My personal spiritual practice is centered in a daily session of my Laban/Bartenieff-inspired modern dance technique, and in the regular schedule of rehearsals through which I prepare for my next series of performances. Making dances and sharing them with the young artists who will perform them and the audiences who choose to witness them is a challenging but spiritually-uplifting process. It is wholly positive and life-affirming. In these troubled times, when both corporations and governments are manipulating us with distortions of the truth, I value the absolute truth I find in the body and in movement more profoundly than ever.

Bill Evans, Abbey Germano, Leah Fox and other SUNY Brockport dance majors in *Together Through Time*, February, 2005.
Photograph by Jim Dusen

Bill Evans and SUNY Brockport dance majors in *Together Through Time*, February, 2005. Photograph by Jim Dusen

Jana Dufort, Catherine DeAngelis, Janet Forward, Alison Earl, Amy McDonald, Amy Rance, Adrienne Wilson, Courney Andrews, Kimberly Jacob, Matt Winans, Bill Evans, Leah Fox, Stephanie Vertichio, Kelly Quinn, Mary Brutvan and Abbey Germano in *Together Through Time*, February, 2005.
Photograph by Jim Dusen

Appendix I

Brief Biography

BILL EVANS IS AN INTERNATIONALLY KNOWN PERFORMER, CHOREOGRAPHER AND teacher of modern dance and rhythm tap dance, as well as an artistic director, movement analyst and writer. He has a BA in English and ballet and an MFA in modern dance from the University of Utah (Salt Lake City). He is a Certified Laban/Bartenieff Movement Analyst (Integrated Movement Studies, Seattle) and a Certified Movement Analyst (Laban/Bartenieff Institute for Movement Studies, New York).

Evans has studied with and/or performed professionally in the works of many leading ballet, tap, jazz and modern dance master teachers and choreographers, including Willam Christensen, Jack Cole, Viola Farber, Peggy Hackney, Betty Jones, José Limón, Murray Louis, Matt Mattox, Donald McKayle, Daniel Nagrin, Alwin Nikolais, Ruth Page, Anna Sokolow, Fred Strickler, Shirley Ririe, Patricia Wilde and Joan Woodbury. He has performed in all fifty states and throughout Canada and Mexico, as well as in many other countries, including Australia, England, Finland, France, Germany, Hungary, India, Italy, Ireland, Japan, New Zealand, Norway and Russia.

He was artistic director of the internationally-acclaimed Bill Evans Dance Company for 30 years (1975 – 2004). This professional company was the most-booked dance company in the U.S. for several years, under the auspices of the National Endowment for the Arts Dance Touring and Artist in the Schools Programs. Evans has directed annual summer dance intensives for teachers and performers since 1976, and he founded the Evans Modern Dance Technique Certification Program in 2002.

He is on the permanent guest faculty of the Professional Program of Winnipeg's Contemporary Dancers and was previously artistic director of Winnipeg's Contemporary Dancers and the School of Contemporary Dancers. He is former director of the Dance Theatre Seattle School of Modern Dance, as well as former artistic coordinator of the Repertory Dance Theatre (Salt Lake City).

He is currently serving as visiting professor/guest artist in the State University of New York College at Brockport Department of Dance. He is professor emeritus in the Department of Theatre and Dance at the University of New Mexico (Albuquerque) and was an associate professor and director of modern dance at Indiana University (Bloomington), a visiting professor of dance at the University of Washington (Seattle) and an assistant professor of modern dance at the University of Utah (Salt Lake City).

Evans has choreographed more than 200 works for more than sixty dance organizations throughout the world and been awarded the Guggenheim

Fellowship, numerous grants and fellowships from the National Endowment for the Arts and more than seventy other awards from public and private arts agencies in the United States and Canada. He has choreographed three original works (2000, 2001 and 2003) under the National College Choreography Initiative supported by grants from Dance USA and the National Endowment for the Arts.

He was named Scholar/Artist of the Year by the National Dance Association in 1997 and was awarded the New Mexico Governor's Award for Excellence in the Arts in 2001. He received the Albuquerque Arts Alliance Bravo Award for Excellence in Dance in 1997 and 2003. He was voted one of the three top American tap dance artists (with Savion Glover and Brenda Bufalino) in the 2004 *Dance Magazine* Readers Poll. In July 2005, he was selected for the Lifetime Achievement Award by the National Dance Education Organization.

He has provided leadership for dance education as an officer in the National Dance Association (NDA) and a member of the board of directors of the National Dance Education Organization (NDEO), for which he produced an annual conference in Albuquerque in October, 2003.

He is in the process of writing a textbook on Evans Modern Dance Technique and a textbook for secondary schools on dance technique and performance. He is the subject of *The Legacy: Bill Evans, Reaching Out from the Regional Southwest*, by Jennifer Noyer, with accompanying videotape by Rogulja Wolf. He has published two videotapes, has two more in production and is the subject of a recently published video interview, *Dance On: Bill Evans*.

Evans has published 15 articles in professional dance journals and magazines and a chapter, "Teaching Movement Analysis," in the book Teaching Dance Studies, edited by Judith Chazin Bennahum and published by Routledge Press. He has been the subject of feature articles in numerous national and international publications, including the October, 2003 issue of *Dance Magazine*.

For more information, visit www.billevansdance.org.

Appendix II

Acceptance Speech
New Mexico Governor's Award for
Excellence and Achievement in the Arts
Dance/Choreography

Palace of the Governors
Santa Fe, New Mexico
September 2001
by Bill Evans

THE CATACLYSMIC EVENTS OF SEPTEMBER 11TH MADE ME PROFOUNDLY GRATEFUL
to have been able to live most of my life through the art of dance. I perceive dance
artists and educators to be uncommonly generous, life-affirming and peace-loving
people. We recognize that there is no life without movement and that movement is
the common bond among all peoples on the planet. We understand that by going
inside the body-mind and witnessing and affirming the incredible miracle of life, we
acknowledge our oneness with all other members of the human race, all other life
forms. We are thus able to put aside superficial differences and to bridge polarities.

Since long before last September 11, I have recognized a crisis in our
society and throughout much of our world: As Developmental Movement
Therapist Bette Lamont says, "We as a culture have become so impressed with
our technology that we have forgotten the body—to our peril." (B. Lamont,
personal communication, June 18, 2001) Ms. Lamont and another good friend,
Anne Green Gilbert, the well-known pioneer in creative movement education,
have shared with me their concerns about a society that does not move enough
and does not understand the value of movement for our children.

For countless generations, babies have used their time on the floor (on their
bellies) to explore and fulfill developmental movement patterns. In recent years
parents have been reluctant to give their children that time on their bellies due to
the fear of Sudden Infant Death Syndrome. (While it is true that babies should
not be put to sleep on their bellies, it is also true that they require supervised
playtime on their bellies everyday.) Most young children in our society today
spend inordinate amounts of time in equipment designed to keep them safe and
to make their parents' busy lives more efficient, such as car seats, play pens, exer-
saucers, jolly jumpers and walkers.

Bette Lamont and Anne Green Gilbert refer to such children as "bucket
babies." Bette explains that,

> *During the first year of life, 50% of the child's brain is organized. During the*
> *second year, the next 25% is organized. (The key to that neurological organization—the*
> *evolution of the central nervous system between birth and 6 to 8 years—is movement.)*
> *As we grow from first fetal squiggles to upright walking, and movement becomes more*
> *complex, it creates a more and more complex brain. It can be argued that it is not the*
> *brain that is moving the body, but the body that is evolving the brain.* (B. Lamont,
> personal communication, June 18, 2001)

Since the brain organizes itself through movement, children who are unable
or who are not allowed to completely fulfill developmental movement patterning

may enter the world with deficits in their abilities to lead full lives. Over the past few decades movement educators and therapists have witnessed huge increases in learning, behavior, motor and social problems in the children with whom they work. As Lamont says, "babies who are not allowed to move in a full way become the children who are supporting the multibillion dollar Ritalin industry, who fill our special education programs, our juvenile justice centers." (B. Lamont, personal communication, June 18, 2001)

Twenty-five years ago, during the days of the National Endowment for the Arts Artists in the Schools Program, my company and I worked frequently in elementary schools. I usually preferred third graders and often worked with the same students daily for four weeks in a single school year. As I recall, there were usually two or three children in a class who had difficulty learning and were hard to control. Bette Lamont says that these words now describe 30% to 50% of the children she sees when she goes into schools. "Half of these students are on drugs and the other half are driving the teachers crazy." (B. Lamont, personal communication, June 18, 2001)

Many people in our society today have very limited movement lives. Parents, teachers, administrators and legislators who seldom move do not understand the necessity of movement for our children. I tell our University of New Mexico dance majors, who will become the state's dance teachers of tomorrow, that they are the key to creating whole human beings in this new century. They need to give their students the time and guidance they require to fully explore their fundamental human movement patterns. They need to demand the scientific research that will quantify the role of movement on the development of the brain. The abundant anecdotal evidence collected by movement educators and therapists needs the support of hard science, so that the importance of movement activities in the lives of our children will be honored and supported by funding bodies, legislators, administrators and parents.

I plead with all of you to continue to encourage the development of dance and movement programs in our pre-K through 12 schools in every way possible. It is my profound hope that the age-old traditions of the indigenous peoples in our home state of New Mexico, who celebrate community and life's sacred events through movement and music, can become models for us all. It is my profound hope that we can foster developmental movement education as the birthright of every child in our culture, and that by so doing we can help to create a healthier, more organized and more civil society.

Contact information: Bette Lamont, MA/DMT, Therapy Director, Developmental Movement and Education Center, 12341 Lake City Way NE, Suite 201, Seattle, WA 98125

Appendix III

1997 National Dance Association Scholar/Artist Lecture

Teaching What I Want To Learn
By Bill Evans

[This Scholar/Artist lecture was delivered to the National Dance Association General Assembly in St. Louis, Missouri (March 1997). The American Alliance of Health, Physical Education, Recreation and Dance (AAHPERD) published it as a booklet and it was also published in a modified version in Contact Quarterly, *Summer/Fall, 1999, Volume 24, Number 2, pages 43–51.]*

Introduction

I am deeply moved to have been named the National Dance Association Scholar/ Artist and wish to express my heartfelt thanks to Penelope Hanstein and the other NDA members who supported my nomination for this honor. I would also like to thank Don Halquist and Debra Landau, members of the Bill Evans Dance Company, who will complement my delivery of this lecture with their beautiful dancing, and my mother Lila Snape Evans and my daughter Thaïs Evans Densley, who have traveled from Utah to support me this morning.

I would like to talk today about the teaching of dance technique as I perceive it at this point in a long, challenging and satisfying journey. Dancing and teaching have been at the very core of my existence since I was a child, and I profoundly value this opportunity to address these subjects before a group of beloved peers, colleagues and future dance artist/educators.

As I have reflected during the past several weeks on what I would most like to say on this topic, several phrases which capture essential beliefs have kept returning to my consciousness: first, "dance is primarily an activity of the human spirit"; second, "I teach what I want to learn"; third, "technique is not working if it shows"; and fourth, "everyone has the right to experience dance." I would like to organize my words under these headings.

The Human Spirit

Several months ago, when asked to select a tentative title for a then unwritten lecture, I decided upon "Dance Technique—Enrichment of Human Movement Potential or Cultivation of Aberrant Behavior." As a professor in a university dance major program, it is often my task to guide students in replacing movement behaviors that are not serving their best interests, with some that might more appropriately do so. I perceive that most of the students who enroll in our program have chosen dance as a major avenue of expression because of a spiritual quest. By the time I have the opportunity to work with them, however, the spiritual aspect of their dancing has often receded. I perceive that they have mostly been trained from a quantitative point of view, that they have been asked to meet externally measurable, idealized standards—rather than having been encouraged to voyage inside their bodies and minds to discover what goals might be realistic and might help them function more effectively within themselves and in the world.

I chose dance—or, rather, dance chose me—because I rejected the competitive team sports which as a child I was being forced to experience. I was not interested in learning the rules or skills of baseball, football and basketball, in which there was a right and wrong way to accomplish each prescribed task, in which one was either a winner or a loser. And yet I loved moving. Even though I grew up in the farming village of Lehi, Utah, in the 1940's, where the only dance people participated in was folk, square or ballroom; I discovered tap dance through Hollywood movie musicals at age three and was creating my own dances and performing them for friends and relatives by age five. My parents purchased a portable record player and several 78 rpm records of such tunes as "Cruising Down the River on a Sunday Afternoon" and "I Love You a Bushel and a Peck." We had a 3-foot by 6-foot strip of linoleum under an archway between the living room and dining room rugs which became my studio and stage, where I would spend hours a day making up dances and teaching them to my younger sister whenever she was willing. My spirit soared at these times. I began to discover who I was and how I could celebrate being alive.

I had few physical skills and no information about the proper way of performing tap dance steps, but I was transformed by this participation in rhythmic sound and movement from a lost little boy who didn't fit in to a young artist able to connect to the universe through the age-old rhythms recorded on those 78 discs and through the audiences in my mind who were sitting in movie houses admiring my performances. I was discovering my way of being fully alive.

My parents had been reluctant to encourage my dancing, thinking that it was a phase I would eventually pass through. When they refused to buy me tap shoes I discovered that I could make sounds on the floor by holding my older brother's marbles under my bare toes. By the age eight and a half, such determined behavior on my part convinced them to allow me to take dancing lessons. My father found a retired vaudevillian hoofer who taught once-a-week hour-long classes in his basement in Salt Lake City. Charles Purrington was about to begin a new class in which there would be other boys (a prerequisite established by my father). Mr. Purrington was 72 years old and legally blind, but he introduced me to a magical world of flaps, shuffles, Buffalo steps, time steps, *pas de bourrées, changements* and *balancés*. I was in heaven. I practiced these steps wherever I went—on the street, going to and coming from school, waiting in lines when running shopping errands, in my parents' café and in my grandfather's pool hall, where I would perform a tap improvisation for anyone who dropped a nickel in the jukebox and gave another to me.

Throughout these early years of training I was fortunate that my teachers (first Charles Purrington and then his daughter June Purrington Park, who had been trained in Hollywood by Ernest Belcher, Marge Champion's father) emphasized the learning and performing of dances in a whole-body, integrated way, rather than focusing on rules or "proper" lines, shapes or positions. The rhythms we made and how we communicated to an audience were more important than how we looked. We didn't really study "technique" so much as "dancing," in various styles, such as tap, ballet, European character dance and flamenco. These teachers encouraged my passionate involvement in both classes and performances, and my self-esteem, which—because I had rejected sports in a sports-oriented family and community—had been extremely low for most of my young life, was enhanced by the positive responses I received from parents, teachers and classmates. We experienced the essence of dance, I believe, as it has been practiced by all cultures in all times. This was not high art, of course, but it gave added meaning to our lives and connected us to each other and to the music and dance icons of our popular culture. I rearranged and choreographed dances and performed them at church socials, weddings and various gatherings of clubs and civic organizations throughout our valley. I began to find my way of experiencing and reflecting my world and my place in it, of expressing my wonderment for the miracle of life.

I had barely begun to learn these steps myself when I started organizing classes after school in the bedroom I shared with my sister and brother, where I would teach a few willing classmates from the Lehi Elementary School the steps I had learned in Salt Lake City as well as some I was inventing myself. By age thirteen, I was teaching several dance classes a week in American Fork, where a high school friend of my mother had opened a studio and invited me to teach the more advanced students. At age fourteen, I choreographed my first major production, *Snow White and the Seven Dwarfs*, for performances in the American Fork High School auditorium, with live music and with sets and props that I made myself.

These untroubled days were not to last, however, because I was approaching adulthood and needed, I believed, to seek professional training if I were to seriously pursue a career as a dancer.

At age fifteen, I enrolled in the academy of a famous ballet master and choreographer who had recently moved to Salt Lake City. This remarkable man was particularly successful at training male dancers who went on to make differences in the world and I found myself in a group of young men from throughout the western United States who had come to Utah to study with this celebrated teacher. I met boys of my approximate age from cities and towns in Montana, Hawaii, Alaska, and Washington state who had also grown up as the only boy they knew who wanted to be a dancer. It was reassuring to be with others like me.

It was also in some ways upsetting. I discovered that my body was mostly "wrong." I did not close my fifth positions all the way. I did not "wrap" my foot around my ankle in *sur le cou de pied,* nor "bevel" it in *arabesque*, in which my knee always looked incorrectly bent. In short, even though I knew every step in the book, had excellent rhythm, was a "quick study" and communicated successfully with audiences, my feet and knees, specifically, and other body parts generally, did not look right, and, therefore, I did not look right. Therefore—I felt—I was wrong. I was entranced by my teacher's remarkable charisma, charm, energy, passion and physical strength, but it was his opinion of my feet and knees, which most concerned me. I became obsessed with conquering them and forcing them to create the "right" positions and lines. I wanted desperately to please my new teacher who tried to accelerate my improvement by verbally humiliating me in front of the other students and—occasionally—by hurling his long black cane across the studio toward my "sickled" feet. I determined that my knees would become straight and my fifth positions completely closed, no matter how long it took.

Even though I eventually succeeded in this quantitative pursuit, the quality of my dancing, my self-esteem and my spiritual life went through a gradual deterioration. Many of my fellow dance students were able to thrive in this atmosphere, but it did not meet my needs. I discovered that my world of dance had become as competitive as the world of sports, which I had rejected, that there were winners and losers here too, and that when I looked wrong I was a loser.

If a student is continuously encouraged to focus on how she or he falls short of making "perfect" body lines or positions, his or her spirit can be broken. I believe that a student whose spirit has been crushed in the process of learning a dance technique has gained skill at too great a price and cannot experience dance in a full and satisfying way. As Linda MacRae-Campbell writes in an article entitled *Whole Person Education* (1988, 16), "Emotions inhibit or facilitate learning.... and performance increases with cooperation not competition." I believe that the body has ways of knowing and communicating essential truths about what it is to be human that can be blocked if a dancer's mind tells him or her that his or her body is not good enough. I believe that dancing that does not honor and reveal the unique spirit of the individual is in fact aberrant, because the very urge to dance comes from the need to express with the whole of ourselves a spiritual statement that is otherwise inexpressible.

I believe that the limited and highly repetitive nature of movement material executed in many codified ballet, modern and jazz technique classes can create aberrant beings who lose their kinesthetic relevance for and connection to their audiences. Many traditional dance technique class practices have resulted in distortions of efficient neuromuscular patterning. For example, I often tell students in my classes that one can go through an entire, successful lifetime without ever doing a single *passé* (placing the toes of the foot of the gesturing leg—usually outwardly rotated at the hip joint—against the back or side of the knee of the supporting leg). Nonetheless, students in most classical, modern or jazz technique classes will execute between thousands and hundreds of thousands of such actions during the course of their dance training. Because early creators of European classical dance styles found this position "beautiful," the *passé*, has been incorporated into our theatrical dance training ever since. A similar but different action, a full flexion of the gesturing hip joint with the same knee flexed, especially when the legs are in neutral rotation, was considered "ugly," and has been avoided, even discouraged, throughout the history of the training of dancers in our European-based theatrical forms.

Ironically, the "beautiful" *passé*, when practiced disproportionately to other possible actions of the leg, can cause neuromuscular imbalances and over-use injuries of the superficial anterior thigh muscles, which can become prime movers rather than more appropriate auxiliary muscles in hip flexion and outward rotation. The practice of the "ugly" full flexion, however, can strengthen the iliopsoas muscle, encouraging it to remain the efficient prime mover in full hip flexion and increasing the likelihood that in this same position the six deep lateral rotator muscles will remain the efficient prime movers in outward femoral rotation. This full flexion of the hip joint is, in fact, one of the fundamental human activities through which the cross-lateral pattern of total body organization is developed as the child learns to crawl contra-laterally. I find that my body needs to invest regularly in this full-range action of the hip joint to maintain core-distal connectivity and balanced strength and flexibility. Other "ugly" gestures or positions, such as extension of the hip of the gesturing leg toward the right back high, middle, or low corners of the kinesphere, demeaned in my early professional training as "looking like a doggie at a hydrant," were also avoided by such early arbiters of acceptable movement materials for inclusion in dance technique classes. Because these rules of body line and position were determined from the outside in, initially by how well they helped to display costumes and jewelry, the body's well-being was not an important consideration. Rather, the decision makers in our European-based cultures dismissed the body and its ways of knowing. This was, of course, consistent with the centuries-old philosophical tradition of deeming the body as the seat of base "animal" needs and instincts, inferior to the higher attributes of the mind. The result of this denial of the ways humans learn and know through the senses resulted in the imposition of postures and movement practices upon the body externally in accordance with ideas about what is and is not "beautiful."

Information not available to the founders of such traditions has allowed me to value the beauty of a well-functioning body in tune with its connection to all other animals and life forms on our planet and the healthful, regenerative ways of moving that can develop from such a perspective.

Much has been said and written in recent decades about the unfortunate "objectification" of the body in our culture through beauty pageants, advertising, entertainment and pornography. I believe that dance teachers, choreographers, critics, audiences and even dancers themselves are often inadvertently responsible for treating the body as an object, of denying the relevance of thoughts, sensations, feelings, injuries and individual structural, emotional and psychological differences, of failing to see the whole person. As Linda MacRae-Campbell says:

> *A stimulating and loving environment enhances learning through the human intelligence, which includes...kinesthetic, visual, musical and intra- and interpersonal elements.... We now know that it is mandatory to incorporate the body, the mind, the feelings, the social and intuitive dimensions of the individual in the learning process.... and [that] the willingness to confront emotional issues not only benefits learning, it also influences self-image, the single most important factor in determining an individual's success in any endeavor in life. (1988, 17)*

Despite the fact that I had found my early love affair with dance replaced by a struggle to become what I could not be, I persevered. I believed that those in authority—because they had been professionally successful—must know what was best for me. Since I was unable to make appropriate pictures with my body, it seemed somehow fitting that I should be verbally abused, that I should have to struggle against my body's deficiencies and endure physical pain.

In 1969, however, after almost 15 years of training in major ballet, modern and jazz styles of dance technique—which I continued to approach with full emotional and physical passion—determined to gain control of the skills that would help me express my choreographic message to the world—I found my 29-year-old body chronically injured. I suffered unrelenting pain in the lumbar spine; I experienced immobility in the cervical spine as a result of a large mound of protective tissue that had developed to shield my neck joints from percussive stretching exercises which required rolling rapidly through a position in which the entire weight of my body was placed on the cervical vertebrae; and I endured chronic knee pain, which had been misdiagnosed and treated for years by several medical professionals as tendonitis. (It was in fact, I later discovered, *chondromalacia*, softening of the patellar cartilage, resulting from lateral/medial muscle imbalance in my quadriceps and from inappropriate outward rotation of the tibia at the knee joint.)

At this point, fearing that my dancing years might already be behind me, I resolved not to take any more technique classes until I figured out for myself what my body needed. For the first time since I had entered the world of "dance instruction through intimidation," a phrase that characterized so much of the serious dance teaching practiced at that time, I decided to take control of my own dance training. I had once been in touch with a body wisdom, I reasoned, which had allowed me to learn quickly, dance expressively and find deep satisfaction in moving. I had gradually become consumed by my body's limitations, as pointed out for me by numerous skilled, successful, well-meaning but tradition-bound technique teachers, and had tried to overcome these perceived deficiencies from the outside in through force and hard work. I wanted to start over, to figure out from the inside what movement patterns would be safe, healthful and regenerative to re-pattern into my neuromuscular system.

Fortunately, I had been given a hiatus from the Repertory Dance Theatre, the professional company of which I was then a full-time member, to travel to West Berlin to create a new work for the German Opera Ballet. While there, I spent several hours each day alone in a huge empty opera house studio, exploring simple gestures, postures and weight shifting activities, trying to figure out what instinctive gifts had enabled me to be such a successful tap dancer as a child and how I could apply that information to my activities as a professional, adult modern dancer. I began to accept the fact that I had learned to hate my body for what I was not, and I started a long process of accepting the realities of my physical structure and of respecting my body's messages to my mind. I discovered that my body would tell my mind what I needed if I would just pay attention to it. I became aware of patterns of breath-holding and permanent contractions in certain large, superficial muscle groups. I began to experiment with various mental images that could guide me to sensations of greater ease, fuller flow, more joint freedom, and eventual changes in muscle composition toward more symmetrical balance and healthier tone.

I was encouraged by early breakthroughs in this process of looking inside and acknowledging and validating what I discovered there, and the world inside—the integrated world of sensation, feeling, mind and spirit—gradually became available to me once again.

I became aware that my early tap dancing had included liberal use of what the Laban system calls "Shape Flow," breath-supported changes in the size and shape of the abdominal and thoracic cavities in support of gestural and postural activities. I began to incorporate the relaxed and natural Shape Flow qualities of the tap dancer (for which I then had no specific name) into my modern dance classroom and choreographic movement patterns whenever I sensed or felt that doing so might be to my advantage. In 1969, that was a radical addition to the modern dance vocabulary, which had been developed by an earnest generation of pioneering artists struggling to have movement taken seriously as profound communication, not mere entertainment. I discovered that my tap technique had encouraged a releasing of the superficial muscles surrounding the hip joint—a balanced use of the whole leg and foot by establishing what I eventually learned was a harmonious rhythm between the psoas and hamstrings as major initiators of femoral flexion and extension. I sensed a need to go "beyond *passé*," to full hip flexion of the gesturing leg, and as I patterned the "Evans passé" (as this action was called by some of my students) into my classes and choreography, I found a deeper strength and control for hip flexion and a greater range of motion in *développés*. I discovered that by replacing the over-reliance on the quadriceps and gluteals that I had developed as a ballet and modern dancer with a fuller use of the smaller, deeper muscles closer to the bone, I could find within a modern dance vocabulary the joint mobility and qualities of lightness and free flow that had characterized my early tap dancing. As I incorporated these sensed, felt and intuited changes into my ways of moving in modern dance technique class, I began a process of body-mind healing that has continued to this day. As MacRae-Campbell tells us:

> *Scientific research in neurology, psychology and education has etched expanded images of what it means to be human.... [There is an] unlimited capacity for lifelong learning...and adults and children learn what has personal relevancy.* (16)

I was learning with excitement and depth because I was finally admitting that my personal needs and awarenesses were relevant. Because of this process, I now believe that I should not only tell a student what is "wrong," but that I should stress what choices could more appropriately serve his or her needs, as he or she helps to define them.

Teaching What I Want to Learn

My mentor and friend, Virginia Tanner, invited me in 1968 to teach twice-weekly technique classes to her advanced students—about fifteen preteens and teens who had been trained since early childhood in her system of creative movement. In the Tanner studio, I had the best laboratory I can imagine for the exploration and development of a new approach to the teaching of dance technique. I was able to work with this same group of young people over a period of five years, as they passed from junior high through high school and into college. Some of these young people even entered the Modern Dance Department at the University of Utah (U of U) as students when I became a full-time assistant professor there in 1974, enabling me to teach them for another two years.

These young people had not studied "technique" in any conventional way, and yet they moved fully, confidently, creatively and expressively. I made an early decision never to tell them that anything I requested of them was "difficult." I had the intuitive wisdom to really look at them, to study carefully the results of the movement activities I requested of them and led them through, and to learn from them. Among these students were several exceptionally dedicated and gifted dancers, including Debbie Poulsen, who danced in my own Bill Evans Dance Company for 15 years, Tina Masaka who performed with Repertory Dance Theatre (RDT) through 1996, Mimi Silverstein, who danced with RDT into the early 1990's, Jackie Lynn Bell, who became an internationally successful teacher and choreographer and Ann Brunsvick Brown (Virginia's niece, who had been pretty much ignored until I was able to help her discover and reveal a profound body wisdom from which we all learned enormously), who has established her own successful children's schools and companies in several locations.

These extraordinary young people, and the exceptional trust and support I received from Virginia Tanner, provided me an opportunity I would never have had otherwise to learn what I needed to know through the process of teaching. I would often instruct through verbal images, as another mentor, Elizabeth R. Hayes, had encouraged me to do, rather than by demonstrating. I would then watch carefully as these beautiful young artists interpreted my images in ways that continually amazed me, with naturalness, ease and whole body-mind commitment. I was guided in this process by the words of Margaret N. H'Doubler, who had mentored Betty Hayes and with whom I had studied on several occasions. In *Dance, A Creative Art Experience,* she said:

> *In building technique, then, we should try not to thwart and block the familiar reaction tendencies, but to release them in order that they may contribute to and co-operate with the goal-aiming efforts of the mind. If the aim is not uppermost, spontaneity will be lost, because of distrust in 'instinctive inspiration.' Organic unity between inner and outer must not be destroyed. New forms should mean growth within the life pattern, not destruction of it. (1957, 93–94)*

It was from these young dancers that I finally learned for myself how to access a full range of kinespheric space, free flow and dynamic phrasing. Many of them remain my friends and colleagues, and I remain enduringly in their debt.

It has been my practice ever since to emphasize in my teaching not only those awarenesses and skills that I have accomplished and that have served me, but also those perceptions and skills which have eluded me and which I have needed in order to create physical and emotional balance in my own dancing. I find that by asking students to embody a desirable body-mind trait or awareness I am able to more fully embody it myself. By repeating verbal descriptions of actions and images that I feel will encourage desirable change, I learn from students, who most often have fewer levels of learned reflexes to get in the way, how to access and embody such change.

Technique Is Not Working If It Shows

I just finished reviving a work on my dance company that I originally choreographed in 1970 as a tribute to Betty Hayes. Each dancer in this virtuosic nine and a half minute piece is required to execute hundreds of leaps/hops/ jumps, to reveal accurately very specific trace forms and pathways in space and to master extremes of flow and rhythmic precision. However, the piece does not accomplish my intent unless the dancer also appears "natural" and spontaneous. I want this piece to express what it feels like for a "regular" human being to want to "jump for joy," to "burst with excitement." If the dancer colors the movement with aristocratic European attitudes, if he or she denies his or her body's volume or weight or the amount of strength required to execute such challengingly full and vigorous movement, if, in short, he or she is less than fully human, then I believe that the kinesthetic messages around which the piece was made cannot be communicated. We worked for months on this piece, developing the required level of physical conditioning, the understanding of spatial forms and clarity of spatial intent, the rhythmic and dynamic phrasing and the sensitivity of the dancers for one another, and yet—when it was performed—many people in the audience expressed feelings of wanting to "leap up on the stage and join in." They did not feel alienated from these dancers as if they were a different race, but connected to them and kinesthetically drawn into their seemingly spontaneous activity. I was very pleased.

Technique, I feel, should be a tool for enhancement of expression, rather than an end in itself. I admire virtuosity and refined development of physical skills as much as anyone. (At younger ages I loved to leap. In my 57th year I still love to turn, spin and spiral into and away from the floor.) But I also feel that if such skills are developed at the expense of recognizably healthy human functioning, if the skilled dancer loses a spontaneous aliveness in the moment, the very essence of dance can be lost.

I am deeply distressed by the kind of dance training that encourages dancers "not to think, but to do," over and over again, becoming essentially interchangeable clones of each other. Some critics and audiences are intrigued by dancers who seem like a race of thoroughbreds, who are so sleek, so hyper-mobile, so able to create extreme lines and positions that they become unrecognizable as "regular" human beings. I usually find such dancers unable to express a complete qualitative range, and therefore, not able to access their full human potential. Over the past few decades, American dancers in particular have often been encouraged to become extremely thin, to stretch their ligaments way beyond what a normal body would ever require for healthy functioning, and to hyper-extend knees, hips and backs in order to create more and more extreme (and, I think, distorted) lines. When I attend a performance by such dancers, I am sometimes deeply saddened, even when the dancer him- or herself is expressing joy, by what I perceive as a loss of one's most valuable possession, a healthy, integrated wholeness of body, mind and spirit.

I believe that the dance technique teacher should study anatomy, kinesiology and systems of body therapy and movement re-patterning to be able to understand and enhance the human movement potential of his or her students. Art, I believe, is about making connections (between the creator and him/herself, between the creator and his/her environment, and between the creator/performer and his/her audience). Training that distorts the humanity of the dancer diminishes the possibility of making connections to audiences, I believe, and can rob the dancer of his/her identity as a fully functioning, fully expressive member of the human race.

My own abilities to understand my body-mind needs and potentials and those of my students have been greatly enhanced by a study of applied kinesiology, initially under the guidance of Karen Clippinger, a friend who taught in my Seattle-based Bill Evans Dance Company School for several years. Karen helped me understand that, as she said in Principles of Dance Training:

> *An application of scientific principles of training to dance is needed. Close work among the dance, scientific and medical communities is necessary to evaluate old methods and develop new methods. There is much work to be done to sort out the valuable dance principles which have been passed down through generations from the myths. Such a process can only yield better methods of dance training and provide a beginning for more effective injury prevention. (1988, 82)*

My growth as a teacher has also been supported by a study of Irmgard Bartenieff's (movement) Fundamentals and Rudolf Laban's theories of Effort, Shape and Space Harmony. I began to understand this work in 1976 when Peggy Hackney, an accomplished dancer and leading Laban/Bartenieff specialist, joined my dance company, and have continued over the years by learning from such Laban-trained professional colleagues as Gregg Lizenbery, with whom I danced for 18 years, and Janet Hamburg, who taught in the Bill Evans Summer Institutes of Dance from 1985 through 1995. These studies in applied kinesiology and Laban/Bartenieff Movement Analysis have given me contexts within which to understand and verbal language with which to communicate the discoveries from my inner world.

I have begun a more recent study of Bonnie Bainbridge Cohen's theories of Body-Mind Centering. By studying the evolutionary developmental movement patterns of the fetus and infant, I have become better able to understand the basic patterns of body-mind organization that serve or fail to serve us throughout our lives. By viewing dance technique as integrated human behavior rather than some kind of specialized, rarefied, exclusive or elite activity, I have been able to make connections between dancing and living at every level.

Linda Hartley, in *The Wisdom of the Body Moving, An Introduction to Body-Mind Centering*, articulates my own experience when she says:

> *...my instinct told me I was 'all up in the air.' I needed to place my feet firmly on the ground and relocate myself clearly in my body. I began to dance as a means to both embody and express who I am. I found I was also on the path of knowing, in a new way, that which I am. As I explored ways of making deeper contact with my body, my body was teaching me a new awareness of myself. (1995, xxii)*

As my teaching practices have evolved, I have tried to reframe priorities, goals, methods and materials I emphasize in dance technique courses in the contexts revealed by such inspired leaders as Clippinger, Hackney, MacRae-Campbell and Cohen. At the same time I have been careful not to lose contact with my own body's wisdom and the style of movement which sprang uniquely from it and which is my personal contribution to the greater language of dance. I am gratified by the accomplishments of students who have taken my courses in recent years, and, as always, I continue to learn from them the true profundities of the information and theories I pass on to them.

Everyone Has The Right To Experience Dance

In the past few years, I have produced performances by the Evans Dance Company that have included diverse populations of dancers and musicians including: young and old (from eight to 72); disabled and non disabled; and untrained or trained (in modern, ballet, tap, clog, flamenco, African gum boot, Irish, jazz, ballroom, Mexican folkloric, East Indian or Native American styles). These opportunities have allowed me to understand even more fully that dance is indeed an activity of the human spirit, that free, full, dramatic, engaging, dynamic and expressive dancing can take place with no reference to a particular "technique" or specific skills or abilities, and that the study of technique and acquisition of skills can, in fact, be detrimental to one's ability to be fully expressive of what it is to be human if those pursuits do not honor organic needs and differences.

I believe that every child in our culture has the right to know his/her body from the inside out in the profound ways that a lifelong study of dance has given me. I am enormously saddened by the low priority that the body and its ways of learning and knowing are given in many of our public and private educational institutions. What is ultimately more important for any of us than the harmonious relationship of the mind and body? How can our society not value and insist upon the kind of whole person education discoverable through dance for every child in our culture? How can we in good conscience withhold such vital opportunities for fullness of being?

I had a brief reunion last year with a woman who had studied in my Seattle school almost 20 years ago. She caught me up on the details of her life and career, which no longer includes dance technique classes. She then thanked me for my teaching and explained how what I helped her understand about scapulo-humeral rotation adds enjoyment to her life every time she washes her back. The comment was more meaningful to me than almost anything she might have said about my dancing or choreography. The thought that I may have helped her find fuller satisfaction in something so fundamental as her daily shower cheered me immeasurably.

At this point, I enter the dance technique studio to remind my students of their connections to the rest of humanity, to the rest of the animal life of the planet, and to the basic compositional elements of our universe. I encourage students to bring their senses, their feelings, their thoughts and their intuition to each facet of the dance technique class experience. I encourage them to explore and acknowledge what they discover in these different parts of themselves and to ask, "What do I want and need, and how can my technique-class discoveries serve me in satisfying these wants and needs."

In December of 1996 I was invited to present a half-day session for the Pennsylvania Association of Health, Physical Education, Recreation and Dance on the subject of my dance technique. In preparing for that challenging and rewarding opportunity, I made a spontaneous and somewhat random list of thoughts—a mind map, as it were—on the teaching of dance technique. Here are some of those thoughts:

Teaching technique is about:

- a passing on, an instilling, a modeling of a set of values.
- self-discovery, understanding choices; what ways of organizing my total body will most effectively help me accomplish the task at hand; what choices will help me move in a healthful, regenerative way?
- balance:
  —of mind and body;
  —of exertion and recuperation;
  —of body parts/muscle groups/body systems;
  —of container and contents;
  —of inner and outer;
  —of stability and mobility; of thought, sensation, intuition and feeling;
  —of modes of movement—body, dynamics, geometric space and shape;
  —of motion factors—attitudes toward weight, space, time and flow;
  —of strength and flexibility;
  —of comfort/harmony and challenge/risk.
- validation of differences; dance technique is a tool through which precious individual differences can be discovered, explored, defined and celebrated.
- understanding elements of style; how can I honor my uniqueness while learning to make the movement choices that will enable me to work effectively in different styles?
- understanding that:
  —the study of dance is a constantly evolving and lifelong process for each of us; this process of gradual change offers profound joy through continual newness;
  —life is change and the opportunity to travel the journey of lifelong change is a precious gift.

Conclusion

I am currently completing a certification course in Integrated (Laban/Bartenieff) Movement Studies. Peggy Hackney, one of my teachers in this program, has articulated a list of questions in regard to the role of the body in learning. She asks:

Are we willing to value:

- pre-conscious knowledge?
- pre-verbal knowledge?
- bodily knowledge?
- body as intelligence?
- expressions of your body as knowledge generators? (1988, 26)

As I have recounted my personal dance technique history in the writing of this lecture, I have come to understand that I did recognize and value these ways of knowing instinctively as a child and that I have gradually come to experience and revalue them as an adult. I am fortunate to have the guidance of colleagues like Ms. Hackney, whose commitment to lifelong learning continues to stimulate me, renew me and make me better able to serve the needs of students.

I began the practice two years ago of asking the students in my technique courses to write me several letters throughout a semester, detailing for me: first, what they consider to be the unique strengths and attributes which serve them in their dancing; second, what goals they have established for the semester to develop new strengths and positive attributes; third, their progress toward those goals; and fourth, a summing up of how they perceive themselves differently at the end of the semester and in what directions they would next like to grow. I always look forward to reading these letters and have often been astounded by the honesty and clarity, the intellectual and emotional depth and the diversity of inner experience and discovery that they reveal to me. More than ever, I am learning from students.

More than ever I realize what a fortunate being I am to be able to engage regularly in such profound exchange with the mostly young artists who are students in the University of New Mexico Dance Program, the artist/colleagues of many ages who comprise the Evans Dance company, and my network of friends throughout the world of dance and dance education. These human beings are willing and able to remain vulnerable, to share with me their thoughts and feelings, and to let me travel with them on their respective and unique journeys through the dance of life.

I am learning what I want to teach.

References

1. Clippinger, K. (1988). "Principles of Dance Training." In Clarkson, P. and Skrinar, M. (Ed.), *Science of Dance Training*. Champaign, IL: Human Kinetic Books, 45–90

2. MacRae-Campbell, L. (1988, Winter). "Whole Person Education." *In Context*, 18, 16–18

3. Hackney, P. (1988, Winter). "Moving Wisdom." *In Context*, 18, 26–29

4. Hartley, L (1995). *Wisdom of the Body Moving*. Berkeley, CA: North Atlantic Books.

5. Hanstein, P. (1995). NDA scholar lecture: "Art making and the art of leadership: an aesthetics of action for change." Reston, VA: American Alliance for Health, Physical Education, Recreation and Dance Publications.

6. H'Doubler, M. (1957). *Dance: A Creative Art Experience*. Madison, WI: University of Wisconsin Press.

Appendix IV

Bill Evans Reunion Concert, August 10, 2002
a review by Cheryl Palonis Adams

*"Have you also learned that secret from the river; that there is no such thing
as time? ...when learned that, I reviewed my life and it was also a river and
Siddhartha the boy, Siddhartha the mature man and Siddhartha the old man
were only separated by shadows; not through reality."*
Siddhartha, *Hermann Hesse*

The brisk, cool Olympic Mountain air dispelled all shadows that August night
in Port Townsend, Washington as time stood still for the universal family of
Bill Evans. As students, dancers, friends and fans gathered in McCurdy Pavilion
Theatre for the Bill Evans Reunion Concert to celebrate and honor Bill Evans,
reality sparkled with excitement, energy and love—love for this incredible man
who has touched so many lives through his artistry, and who has sustained this
extended family through his capacity to nurture and re-ignite relationships.
Those of us who have known Bill for half of our lives, and those who had just
entered the fold, were blessed with a magical evening.

The program opened with the rapturous *Albuquerque Love Song*, the first of
three solos in *Suite Cava*, choreographed by Bill Evans to the exceptional music
of composer and pianist, Michael Cava. Lying in a silent pool of light, Evans
carved his arms in widening circles as though awakening from sleep until he
became upright and the enchanting piano intoned. In a satiny costume, Evans
shimmered, at once enlivened by and united with the space as he spiraled, spoked
and carved the space with clarity. He descended again at the close, folding in
upon himself until the final, vulnerable spreading gesture of his arms; a deeply
moving moment in which Evans abandoned himself to the audience.

In *Dreamweaver*, Linda Johnson-Gallegos, soloist with Bill Evans Dance
Company since 1990, magically articulated every joint like an exquisite fairy-like
creature to the enchantingly playful Cava score. The music and dancer became
one as Johnson-Gallegos embraced each note through mesmerizing arpeggios of
arms and legs. In sweeping body chords, she played like a harpist,advancing and
retreating, weaving a spell.

Don Halquist, like a gossamer plaything of the gods, twirled, twisted,
rotated and extended toward his goal in *Climbing to the Moon*. Halquist, Evans's
partner and soloist with the company since 1985, richly embodies the flavors and
nuances of Evans Technique. In this solo, he appeared in a state of perpetual
motion with one sustained, free breath from which he spread and enclosed and
balanced exquisitely in anticipation. The work ended as Halquist began a series
of spiraling, central turns growing ever faster as the lights faded.

Gail Heilbron, Co-director of Co-Motion Dance in Seattle, performed
Emanating Currents to the haunting music of Komitas Vardapost, Armenian

Folk Music, and Michio Mamiya. In this trancelike work, Heilbron exhibited the virtuosity of her range of movement from the gentle curving of a single hand to the effortless balance of a backward turn in side extension.

Traveling from New Zealand to reunite with Bill after 23 years, Jennifer De Leon of the Poyema Dance Company danced to the music of Caravena in her piece, *Remembering You*. DeLeon's tribute evoked a sense of the Modern Dance Pioneers. She is a wisp of a woman who executed flowing turns, powerful extensions, and graceful falls and rolls with deep emotional commitment.

Holly Bright presented *Night Swim*, choreographed by Deborah Dunn with music by Chopin. Bright, Artistic Director of Crimson Coast Dance Society in Nanaimo, British Columbia, moved with astonishing flexibility as she rolled and piked and somersaulted her way through the imaginary waters. Her tantalizing undulations transported the audience to the place of exhilarating freedom a sea creature must feel in the lunar glow.

Shimmerline—"the spontaneous creative state between contrivance and abandon" was performed by Human Jazz's Christian Swenson. Truly awesome is Christian's vocal range with which he intertwines his intricate movement to create bewildering effects. With masterful articulation of body parts and vocal sounds, Swenson's performance moved from drama to comedy with ease. Marcel Marceau, Bobby McFerrin, an ancient Shaman, an embodiment of the collective unconscious; Swenson shared a mesmerizing work of unparalleled skill.

Evans' *Colony*, danced by Bellingham, Washington's Dance Gallery, is a piece inspired by the Maori people with whom Evans had worked in New Zealand. *Colony* explores the duality of the lives of the Maoris under British rule. These native people's spirits were confined within the restrictive Victorian mores, shown most notably in the clothes they were required to wear. Seven dancers span the stage, seated sedately in chairs, attempting conformity of movement. However, in spite of their outward appearance, their inner sense of self and culture is destined to emerge. The repetitious, driving beat of the score evoked empathy for these people—imprisoned by the monotony of a foreign culture. Dance Gallery's performers created superb images of these multi-dimensional Maoris—each dancer illuminating a unique essence.

Evans and Halquist teamed with Charlene Curtiss, Director of Light Motion, and Joanne Petroff, Artistic Director of Whistlestop Dance, in *Take the "A" Train* and *Mood Swing*, both choreographed by Evans to the music of Glenn Miller. In *Take the "A" Train*, the foursome, men in white jacketed tuxes, women in vibrant period dresses, performed a kind of slow-motion caricature of the time. With painted-on smiles, they paraded like animated pictures from the photogravure. All of the movements were highly amusing, especially Halquist's multiple jumps landing in splits from which he emerged coyly smug.

Curtiss, Halquist and Petroff formed a dynamic trio in their rendition of *In the Mood*. Curtiss's wheelchair became a fourth, essential member of the company as the choreography reflected the spins and stops and starts of the wheels. The threesome (plus 1) jumped and jived to the Big Band sounds in this playful, feel-good piece.

Founding member of the Bill Evans Dance Company, Shirley Jenkins, touched the audience deeply with her emotional performance of *Around Heaven*, sung by Ray Charles. An angelic vision in flowing white, Jenkins created a sense of soulful abandon as she whirled and spun around the stage reaching to the sky.

Wade Madsen caused riotous laughter and applause with his hypnotic solo to Judy Garland's *I Can't Give You Anything But Love*. A striking figure, center-center, in his undershirt and briefs, Madsen executed a deftly constructed striptease, from meticulously unfastening every imaginary button and tauntingly removing elbow-length gloves to teasingly rolling down his gartered stockings, with superb theatrical aplomb.

Jim Coleman, another founding member of the Bill Evans Dance Company and Co-Artistic Director of Freedman/Coleman Dance Company with his wife, Terese Freedman, made this night a true family affair. They teamed with their children, Zoë and Evan, to perform their work, *Family Pictures*, a true-to-life portrayal of a husband and wife, mother and father, whose lives with children seem never to be their own, but also have immeasurable rewards.

The sound collage accompaniment transported everyone to the often chaotic place known as home. Buried under a pile of stuffed animals, clothes, and children's toys, the parents emerged to dance an intimate moment of connection, difficult to achieve because of family disruptions. The work stunningly portrayed family dynamics—Zoë, the princess; Evan, the son, challenging his relationship with dad. Perhaps the most poignant moment occurred when, after a struggle of wills, Jim lifted Evan and carried him offstage in an emotional embrace.

This timeless evening concluded with a powerful performance by Evans, a tap piece dedicated to William Ferdinand Evans, *Dances for My Father*. As the dance floor was rolled away, Evans shared the history of his tap dancing experiences and the role his father played—from staunch resistor to supportive coach. The work that interweaves images from Bill's life with his father was a masterful display of Evans' incomparable talent as a tap dancer. From the a cappella opening with Evans creating complex rhythms through a travelogue of classic tap steps set to the jazzy sounds of Count Basie, Bill's delight in the art of tap dancing and in his father radiated throughout the audience.

Unfortunately, this extraordinary event had to come to an end. But those fortunate to attend were truly suspended in time.

Appendix V

**Two Reviews That Gave Me Confidence As A Performer,
by Alan M. Kreigsman and Anne Marie Welsh**

THE WASHINGTON POST

January 15, 1976

Alan M. Kriegsman, Dance Critic

Will the real Bill Evans please stand? This amazing dancer-choreographer from Utah, currently in residence at George Washington University, seems to have more disguises than Sherlock Holmes, all wondrously credible and diverting.

His solo recital drew an appreciative audience of several hundred to the Marvin Theater Tuesday night. The program consisted of eight highly contrasted dance monologues, all but two choreographed by himself. Evans, a long-time member of Utah's Repertory Dance Theatre, now directs his own troupe in Salt Lake City and is a frequent guest artist in this country and abroad.

Evans' eclecticism, his penchant for satire, the splendid independence of his limbs and his knife-point shifts of tempo and dynamics all put one in mind of Paul Taylor. But Evans' sleek body lines and way of moving are entirely his own, as is his remarkably deft, resilient technique.

To music ranging from Bach to Glenn Miller to Indian ragas, Evans' choreographic idioms shuttled from poetic abstraction to ironic portraiture to frisky parody to trance-like introspection. As a dancer, he also moved with equal ease from the flippancy of Matt Mattox's "Opus Jazz Loves Bach" to the feverish agitation of an excerpt from Anna Sokolow's "Lyric Suite." Evans' own inventions seemed smart and fluent, but they left one wondering how he might fare with larger compositional structures. There was no question, though, about the abundance of his talent.

SAN DIEGO UNION

Monday, June 3, 1985

Anne Marie Welsh, Arts Critic

Bill Evans has been teaching as a regent's lecturer at UCSD since last week. He has solid reputation as a choreographer and teacher. Of the more than 100 works he has created for ballet and modern companies coast to coast, only three had crossed my path before last night. Those three group pieces had intelligence, wit and good nature to recommend them, though nothing so distinctive they suggested an Evans style. Last night Evans performed two of his own solos at Mandeville Auditorium. As a dancer, he is something special, with a style very much his own. He moves with a sensuous abandon and rhythmic subtlety uncommon among male dancers.

Evans has performed for 20 years, first with ballet, then with modern and finally with his own companies in Seattle and Winnipeg. His own technique looks neither modern, classical, nor some eclectic mix of the two. It's as if he re-thought the whole impulse toward movement for himself and arrived at some rather startling conclusions. Like Isadora Duncan and Erick Hawkins, he seems to center himself in the solar plexus and let the energy move in continuous waves outward. There's nothing sharp, angular or aggressive in his dancing, nothing particularly contemporary, not a drop of salesmanship.

When you watch him, your eyes go not to his handsome face or lovely feet, but to his breastbone, the vulnerable, merely human spot that seems to be guiding him.

His dances were different in character—a tap number that became a character dance, a primal-modern work based on Indian classical dance. "Pop's Rag," set to Scott Joplin piano rags, was a soft-shoe with taps full of rhythmic invention that never slavishly followed the music's syncopated beat. Evans has the familiar tap steps down cold—time steps, buck 'n wings, windmill spins. He dances organically, though, with the nuances of his arms movements, his spiraling torso as interesting as the talking taps. In the end, the number seems a nostalgic tribute from one kind of dancer to those of another age.

"Tin-Tal" was set to music for sarod and tabla by Mahapurush Misra. Here Evans let all his subtle virtuosity show. The work began on the floor, moved broadly through space and closed with a long, spiraling passage in which the hands fleetingly spoke that gestural language of the *mudras*. Contrasts between large and small-scaled motions, fast and slow, up and down, sustained interest in a piece as minimal as its score. Like a dervish or a prophet, Evans absorbed himself in the spirit of movement without the fakery prevalent in so much pop-primal choreography. Instead of hypnotizing the mind, he deepens its awareness.

Appendix IV

Listing of Selected Choreographic Works

(title/composer; city of premier performance; name of company;
    subsequent restagings)

BEDCO: Bill Evans Dance Company;
BERTE: Bill Evans Rhythm Tap Ensemble;
BESD: Bill Evans Solo Dance;
BESID: Bill Evans Summer Institute of Dance

2005
Procession and Aftermath/Pieter Bourke and Lisa Gerrard; Minneapolis; Minnesota
    Dance Educators Coalition
Tenderly/Bill Evans**; Santa Fe, 7th Annual New Mexico Tap Dance Jam
Secrets/Pieter Bourke and Lisa Gerrard; Winnipeg, Canada; Professional Program/
    School of Contemporary Dancers
Rite of Summer/Pieter Bourke, Jan Garbarek and Lisa Gerrard; Port Townsend,
    Washington; Dance Gallery of Bellingham

2004
Just a Few Broken Columns/Silvestre Revueltas; Toronto, Ontario, Canada; Jolene
    Bailie Solo Dance (of Winnipeg, Manitoba, Canada)
Los Conejos Locos/Margarita Lecuona, Alberto Dominguez, Ariel Guzik and
    Juan Garcia Esquivel; Winnipeg, Canada; Professional Program/School of
    Contemporary Dancers
Rhythms of the Earth/Evans**; Albuquerque, New Mexico; Bill Evans Dance Company
    (BEDCO)
Scatap/Evans**; Muncie, Indiana; Ball State University Dance Theatre

2003
Together Through Time/Evans**; Edmond, Oklahoma; Kaleidoscope Dancers,
    University of Central Oklahoma; created under the DanceUSA/National
    Endowment for the Arts National College Choreography Initiative; subsequently
    restaged on SUNY Brockport student dancers
Freddie the Freeloader/Miles Davis; Santa Fe, New Mexico; BEDCO
Cindered Heart/Michael Cava; Seattle, Washington;
    Light Motion Dance Company
Tapadanza/Evans**; Las Cruces; New Mexico State University Dance Program

2002
Songs of Ancient Summer/George Crumb; Albuquerque; BEDCO and TRIP Dance
    Company (of Winnipeg, Canada)
The Space Between our Thoughts/Jack Manno (co-choreographed with Acia Gray);

Albuquerque; BEDCO and Tapestry Dance Company (of Austin, Texas)

Landscapes Idaho! /Brian Smith and Chris Teal; Moscow, Idaho; University of
Idaho Dance Theatre; site-specific work created under the Dance USA/National
Endowment for the Arts National College Choreography Initiative; toured
throughout Idaho (Coeur d'Alene, McCall, Ketchum, Boise, Idaho Falls and Twin
Falls)

Preludes/Frederic Chopin; Albuquerque; University of New Mexico (UNM) Dance
Company

Fusion/Serge Prokofiev; Albuquerque; UNM Dance Company
(co-choreographed with Eva Encinias-Sandoval)

Passionate Steps/J. S. Bach; Miami, Florida (National High School Dance Festival);
Douglas Anderson School of the Arts Dance Company
(of Jacksonville, Florida)

2001

Remembering/J. S. Bach; Jacksonville, Florida; Jacksonville University Dance Theatre;
subsequently restaged on Professional Program/School of Contemporary Dancers
(Winnipeg); Kaleidoscope Dancers, University of Central Oklahoma (Edmond); Dance
Gallery (Bellingham, Washington); UNM Dance Company; BEDCO; Iowa State
University Dance Company (Ames); Kansas University Dance Program (Lawrence);
Susan Koper and Dancers (Muncie, Indiana); Anderson/Young Ballet Theatre
(Anderson, Indiana)

Walkabout/Tanya Gerard, Michael Kott, Jeff Sussman, Robert Thomas; Winnipeg,
Canada; Professional Program/School of Contemporary Dancers; subsequently
restaged on SUNY Brockport student dancers

Heart Songs/J.S. Bach; Fresno, California; Portable Dance Troupe, California State
University at Fresno

Dinner with Charlie/Charles Mingus; Scottsdale, Arizona; Instinct Dance Corps,
Scottsdale Community College

Colony/Tanya Gerard, Michael Kott, Jeff Sussman, Robert Thomas; Bellingham,
Washington; Dance Gallery

Dreamweaver/Michael Cava; Santa Fe; BEDCO; subsequently restaged on
Professional Program/School of Contemporary Dancers (Winnipeg)

I'm Dreaming of Heaven But I Know I Been Wrong/Roy Milton and Charles Mingus;
Santa Fe; BEDCO

Incantations II/Warlen Bassham; Anne Green Gilbert's Kaleidoscope Dance Company;
Seattle

2000

Colloquium/Tanya Gerard, Michael Kott, Jeff Sussman, Robert Thomas; Fresno;
Portable Dance Troupe, California State University at Fresno

Dances for the Inner Child/Sergei Prokofieff; Albuquerque; BEDCO

The Twelfth Day/Schonherz and Scott; Sandia Park, New Mexico; BEDCO

Spirit Walkabout/Tanya Gerard, Michael Kott, Jeff Sussman, Robert Thomas;
    Albuquerque; UNM Dance Company

Miller Time/Glenn Miller and his Orchestra; Port Townsend, Washington; Light
    Motion Dance Company

Sweet Skip/Charlie Parker; Albuquerque; Bill Evans Rhythm Tap Ensemble (BERTE)

Song Without Words/Max Bruch; Provo, Utah; Dancers' Company, Brigham Young
    University

Journey to the Moon/Benoit Jutras; Pioneer Dance Arts; Sequim, Washington

Stand By Your Man/Patsy Cline; Nanaimo, British Columbia; BEDCO

1999

Silver Tones/a cappella; Albuquerque; BERTE

Song for My Father/Horace Silver; Albuquerque; BERTE

It's About Time/Damian Espinosa and Jefferson Voorhees; Albuquerque;
    UNM Dance Company

Three to Twelve/a cappella; Albuquerque; BERTE

Blues Suite/Thelonius Monk, Jon Hendricks and Bobby Timmons; Albuquerque;
    BERTE

Bums on Seats/Duke Ellington; Albuquerque; BERTE

Yes, Indeed! /a cappella; Muncie, Indiana; Ball State University Dance Theatre;
    subsequently restaged on University of Wyoming Dance Company (Laramie) under
    the Dance USA/NEA National College Choreography Initiative; UNM Dance
    Company; BEDCO; Kansas University Dance Program (Lawrence)

Elemental Experience/Adam Crawley, Hans Heintzelman and Michael Lopez; Muncie;
    Ball State University Dance Program

You Go, Girl! /a cappella; Edmond; Kaleidoscope Dancers, University of Central
    Oklahoma

Suite Beethoven/Ludwig van Beethoven; Socorro, New Mexico; BEDCO

Taptacit/a cappella; Socorro, Bill Evans Solo Dance (BESD)

1998

Passionsong/Max Bruch; Albuquerque; UNM Dance Company

Bush Walk/InLaKesh; Louisville, Kentucky; Barking Dog Dance Company

Une Vigile/Gabriel Fauré; Winnipeg, Canada; Professional Program/School of
    Contemporary Dancers

Keep on Tryin' II*/Simon Jeffes; Albuquerque; New Mexico Ballet Company

1997

Devolving Spheres/Carlos Nakai; Port Townsend, Washington; in collaboration with
    Charlene Curtiss, Don Halquist and Joanne Petroff

Pedestrian Package/a cappella; Port Townsend; in collaboration with Charlene Curtiss,
    Don Halquist and Joanne Petroff

Mood Swing/Glenn Miller and His Orchestra; Port Townsend; Light Motion Dance Company

The Nutcracker, Act I/Peter Ilyich Tchaikovsky; Albuquerque; New Mexico Ballet Company

Albuquerque Love Song/Michael Cava (commissioned score); Albuquerque; BEDCO

Los Ritmos Calientes/Dave Brubeck, Enrique Fernandez, Horace Silver; Deming, New Mexico; BERTE; in collaboration with Sara Hutchinson, Skip Randall and Mark Yonally

Climbing to the Moon/Michael Cava (commissioned score); Seattle, Washington; Cava-Parker Dance Company

Isle of View/Simon Jeffes; Bremerton, Washington; Peninsula Dance Theatre

Odyssey/Altan; Everett, Washington; Jackson High School Dancers

Spirit Walk II/InLaKesh; Albuquerque; UNM Dance Company

1996

Saintly Passion/J. S. Bach; Seattle, Washington; BEDCO

Naturescape Unfolding/Brian Eno; Albuquerque; BEDCO

Revisitations/Vincent Persechetti; Albuquerque; BEDCO

Poinciana/Cal Tjader; Kuopio, Finland; BESD

Planctus/Steve Peters; Albuquerque; commissioned by Dance Magnifico—Albuquerque Festival of the Arts; in collaboration with Nora Reynolds Daniel

Cellular Breathing/Taj Mahal; Seattle; Bill Evans Summer Institute of Dance (BESID)

Tribute/ Benoit Jutras; Everett, Washington; Jackson High School Dancers

Incantations/Warlen Bassham (commissioned score); Seattle; Ann Green Gilbert's Kaleidoscope Dance Company

Evocations/Evans**; Rock Springs, Wyoming; Desert Dance Theatre, Western Wyoming Community College

Ceremony of the Springtime Moon/Evans**; Albuquerque; Albuquerque Youth Dance Troupe

Spirit Walk/InLaKesh; El Paso, Texas; Dance Theatre El Paso

1995

Suite Christmas/Irving Berlin; Albuquerque; BESD

Rhythms of the Heart/Jerry Mulligan; Albuquerque; BERTE

Suite Rhythm/Artie Shaw; Madison Wisconsin; Wisconsin Dance Ensemble

Celebration for Paquita/Evans*; Albuquerque; Celebrate Youth Dancers

1994

Pilgrimage/David Yoken and Mikko Mikkla; London, England; Professional Program/London Contemporary Dance School

Winterdance/David Yoken; Turku, Finland; TUTVO Dance Company

Los Perdidos/J. S. Bach; San Luis Potosi, Mexico; BEDCO

Velorio II* (full evening-length version)/Gabriel Fauré (performed live by City Cantabile
    Choir and Orchestra); Seattle; Velorio Project/Strong Wind Wild Horses (modern
    dance company directed by Shirley Jenkins)
Rhythms of the Soul/ Jim Knapp Trio; Seattle; Velorio Project/Strong Wind Wild
    Horses; in collaboration with Shirley Jenkins, Cheryl Johnson and Anthony Peters
How to Name It/Ilaiyaraaja; Albuquerque; BESD
Dance Begun on Christmas Day/Frederic Chopin; Pune, India; BESD

1993

Back At You /original text, vocal and instrumental music and movement in
    collaboration with performance artist Kestutis Nakas and musician John Bartlit;
    Albuquerque; BESD
Incantations for Elizabeth/Evans**; Albuquerque; University of New Mexico Dance
    Company
Rhythm on Tap/Artie Shaw; Albuquerque; Albuquerque Youth Dance Troupe;
    Albuquerque Festival of the Arts
Mingus Amongus/Charles Mingus; Seattle; Strong Wind Wild Horses; subsequently
    restaged on BEDCO
No Mean Feet/Evans**; Kobe, Japan; UNM Contemporary Dance Ensemble
Circular Reverie/Gabriel Fauré; Monterrey, Mexico; Ballett Impulso de Monterrey

1992

Monk Dances/Thelonious Monk; Seattle; Bill Evans and Shirley Jenkins; subsequently
    restaged on BEDCO
Holiday Sweet/Oscar Peterson; Seattle; Bill Evans and Shirley Jenkins
Sentinels/Brian Eno; Albuquerque; BEDCO; commissioned by Dance Magnifico—
    Albuquerque Festival of the Arts
Espiritus de la Tierra/Inti-Illimani/Evans; Albuquerque; Albuquerque Youth Dance
    Troupe

1991

Uncoiled Heart/W. A. Mozart, Albuquerque; BEDCO; commissioned by Dance
    Magnifico—Albuquerque Festival of the Arts
Chantdance/Evans; Albuquerque; Albuquerque Youth Dance Troupe
Danza/Inti-Illimani; Albuquerque; UNM Contemporary Dance Ensemble
Bob's Blues/Robert Tate; Albuquerque; UNM Contemporary Dance Ensemble
Jumpin' With Jefferson/Jefferson Voorhees; Albuquerque; UNM Contemporary Dance
    Ensemble
Velorio/Gabriel Fauré; El Paso, Texas; International Dance Theatre; subsequently
    restaged on: Montclair State University Dance Company (New Jersey); UNM
    Dance Company (two different productions); BEDCO; Ball State University
    Dance Theatre (Muncie, Indiana); Anderson Young Ballet Theatre (Anderson,
    Indiana); Moving Arts Dance Collective (Walnut Creek, California); Sam Houston

State University (Huntsville, Texas); University of Wyoming Dance Company
(Laramie) under the Dance USA/NEA National College Choreography Initiative

1990

Summer's Night Dance/Evans**; Edmond, Oklahoma; Star Dance Swan Contemporary
Dance Theatre
There Was A Boy/Nat "King" Cole; Albuquerque; BESD
Fable/Chris Shultis (commissioned score); Albuquerque; UNM Contemporary Dance
Ensemble
Cuttin' A Rug/a cappella; Albuquerque; UNM Contemporary Dance Ensemble

1989

Round Seven/Jesse Manno; Boulder, Colorado; Colorado Repertory Dance Company
SunRiseDanSet/Simon Jeffes; Edmond, Oklahoma; Star Dance Swan Contemporary
Dance Theatre
Hallowed Halls/Carl Landa; Troy, New York; Emma Willard School Dancers
The Skin Drum/ Albuquerque; UNM Opera Workshop for the National College
Opera Festival
The Rocky Horror Show/ (choreographer and co-director); Santa Fe; New Mexico
Repertory Theatre Company

1988

Flip Side at the Savoy/Duke Ellington; Denton, Texas; Penelope Hanstein and Gail Ziaks
Suite Duke/Duke Ellington; Seattle; Co-Motion Dance Company
BLT Blues/a cappella; Bloomington, Indiana; BESD

1987

Suite Summer/Gregory Ballard (commissioned score); Colorado Springs, Colorado;
BESID; subsequently restaged on Indiana University Dance Theatre
Summer Songs/Sweet Honey in the Rock; Bloomington, Indiana; BESID
Take One-Take Two/Brian Eno and J.S. Bach; Bloomington; Indiana University Dance
Theatre
Heartwind/Simon Jeffes; Baltimore, Maryland; Towson State University Dancers
Suite Benny/Benny Goodman; Salt Lake City; Repertory Dance Theatre (RDT);
subsequently restaged on Southwest Ballet Company (Albuquerque)

1986

In The Beginning/Simon Jeffes; Salt Lake City; RDT
Comes Winter/Evelyn Jensen; Ames Iowa; Iowa State University Dancers
Plainsong/Simon Jeffes; Wichita, Kansas; Mid-American Dance Company
No Laughing Matter/Simon Jeffes; Raleigh, North Carolina;
Meredith College Dancers
Tide Pool/Simon Jeffes; Honolulu, Hawaii; University of Hawaii Dancers

Tres Tangos/Valeria Munnariz Seattle; Co-Motion Dance Company; subsequently
    restaged on Barking Dog Dance Company (Louisville, Kentucky); Eisenhower Dance
    Ensemble (Rochester Hills, Michigan); BEDCO
Shattered Butterflies/Valeria Munnariz; Oakland, California; Mills College Repertory
    Dance Company
Nostalgias/Valeria Munnariz; Santa Fe; Santa Fe Dance Foundation
And That's Final/Simon Jeffes; Denton; Texas Woman's University Dance Faculty
The Fundamental Things Apply/Simon Jeffes; Colorado Springs; BESID

1985

Weathered Wall/Arvo Part; South Hadley, Massachusetts; Five College Dance
    Department Dancers
Side Orders/Simon Jeffes; Harrisonburg, Virginia; Thomson/Trammel Duet Company
Dream Tigers/Hector Villa Lobos; Meadville, Pennsylvania; BEDCO (based on the
    writing of Jorge Luis Borghes, who spoke before the premier performance)
Craps (second movement)/Steve Kim; Salt Lake City; Ririe-Woodbury Dance Company
In A Former Life/Evans; Houston, Texas; Anita Lemon/Chrysalis Repertory Dance
    Company
Soliloquy/Bill Evans**; Salt Lake City; BESD
Dances for My Father/"Count" Basie and His Orchestra; Salt Lake City; BESD
In The Nick of Time/Theolonius Monk; Salt Lake City; BESD

1984

Prairie Fever/Simon Jeffes; Winnipeg; Winnipeg's Contemporary Dancers
Umbre Solstice/Arvo Part; Interlochen, Michigan; Interlochen Arts Academy Dancers
Emily's Dilemma/Gale Ormiston; San Antonio, Texas; Kista Tucker/Dance Art San
    Antonio
From Here to Eternity/Gale Ormiston; Winnipeg; BESD
Grounded Assent/Arvo Part; Middlebury, Vermont; Dance Company of Middlebury
    College

1983

*Origins and Impulses (*later renamed *For Anna)*/Dimitri Shostakovich; Seattle; BEDCO
The New People Too/traditional American Indian poetry; Cincinnati, Ohio;
    Contemporary Dance Theatre
To Be Continued/Simon Jeffes; Provo, Utah; Dancers' Company, Brigham Young
    University
Out of Sorts/Simon Jeffes; Tucson, Arizona; Territory Dance Theatre
Tuesday Morning/Evans** and David Yoken; San Antonio, Texas, Dance Art San Antonio
Calabash Boom/Floyd Williams; Pittsburgh (Pennsylvania) Dance Alloy;
    subsequently restaged on BEDCO
Thoughts on Parting/Scott Cossu; Seattle; BESD

1982

Chartered Flight/Simon Jeffes; Winston-Salem, North Carolina; North Carolina Dance Theatre

Cakewalkin' Babies/Bessie Smith; Seattle; BEDCO

Alternating Current/Simon Jeffes and David Sannella; Seattle: Jim Coleman and Terese Freedman Duet Company; subsequently restaged on BEDCO; Winnipeg's Contemporary Dancers; UNM Dance Company; and Tennessee Dance Theatre, Nashville

Doin' M' Best/Simon Jeffes; Raleigh, North Carolina; Easy Moving Company; subsequently restaged on BEDCO

Keep On Tryin'/Simon Jeffes; Dallas, Texas; Dancers Unlimited Repertory Company

Episodes/David Sannella; Miami, Florida; Fusion Dance Company

Storm Warnings/Simon Jeffes; Detroit, Michigan; Harbinger Dance Company

Passage/Andrej Panufnik; Seattle; BEDCO

This Way and That/Lucinda Lawrence; Champaign-Urbana; University of Illinois Dance Company

1981

Index/Robert Fripp and Brian Eno; Dallas, Texas; BEDCO

Diverse Concerto/Antonio Vivaldi; Chico, California; BEDCO

Sweet and Lovely/Bill Evans; Seattle; BESD

Waltz for Debby/Bill Evans; Seattle; BESD

Le Jazz/Bohuslav Martinu; Seattle; Pacific Northwest Ballet Company

Restless/Wall Matthews (commissioned score); Chicago, Illinois; Lois Royne; subsequently restaged on Linda Lee McAndrew (New York City)

1980

Huntsville City Limits/Steve Kim and David Sannella; Seattle; Christine Sarry and Gregg Lizenbery

Restless Bond/Linda Dowdell; Santa Fe; Lee Connor and Lorn MacDougal/Dances of the High Desert; subsequently restaged on BEDCO

Making the Magic/David Sannella; Seattle; BEDCO; subsequently restaged on UNM Dance Company

Concerto for Tap Dancer and Orchestra/Morton Gould; Seattle; BESD

The Rhode Island Rag/Eubie Blake; Providence, Rhode Island; members of four different professional dance companies in Rhode Island

1979

Craps (first and third movements)/Mark Johnson and Joe LaBarbera; Seattle; BEDCO; subsequently restaged on Ririe-Woodbury Dance Company; Indiana University Dance Theatre; Eisenhower Dance Ensemble; UNM Dance Company; Harvard University Summer Dance Center; Saint Louis (Missouri) Dancers; Professional Program/School of Contemporary Dancers (Winnipeg); Desert Dance Theatre

(Tempe, Arizona); Montclair (New Jersey) State University Dance Company; University of Washington Dance Program (Seattle); Eastern Michigan University Dance Program (Ypsilanti); American Dance Festival at Duke University

Captive Voyage/George Crum; Atlanta, Georgia; Atlanta Contemporary Dance Company

Mixin' It Up/Bill Evans Trio (Bill Evans, Mark Johnson and Joe LaBarbera); Seattle; BEDCO; subsequently restaged on Indiana University Dance Theatre; RDT

The Field of Blue Children/David Sannella; Seattle; Cynthia Gregory and Bill Evans

1978

Impressions of Willow Bay/David Sannella; Seattle; BEDCO

The New London Quadrille/traditional military marches; New London, Connecticut; BEDCO

Double Bill/Bill Evans Trio (Bill Evans, Philly Joe Jones and Mike Moore); Seattle; BEDCO

1977

Conjurations/David Sannella; Seattle; BEDCO; subsequently restaged on San Jose (California) Dance Theatre

Barefoot Boy with Marbles in His Toes/Paul Bley; Seattle; BEDCO

The Ashtabula Rag/Brian Dykstra; Ashtabula, Ohio; BEDCO; subsequently restaged on Several Dancers Core (Atlanta)

1976

Bach Dances/J. S. Bach; Salt Lake City; BEDCO; subsequently restaged at American Dance Festival at Connecticut College and on Five By Two Plus Dance Company (New York City)

I've Got a Gal in Kalamazoo/Glenn Miller and His Orchestra; New London, Connecticut/American Dance Festival; BESD

The Dallas Blues/Bessie Smith; New London/American Dance Festival; BEDCO

Mack and Mabel/ Salt Lake City; dancers chosen in open audition; Pioneer Memorial Theatre

1975

Concerto for Diverse Dancers/Antonio Vivaldi; Salt Lake City; University of Utah Department of Modern Dance

Companion Pieces/Evans; Salt Lake City; RDT

Echoes of Autumn/Andrej Panufnik; Salt Lake City; Ballet West

Summerdance/Evans; Washington, D. C.; Choreo 18; subsequently restaged on University of Nebraska at Omaha Dance Program

End of the Trail/Bill Monroe and Montana Slim; Missoula, Montana; Dance Montana; subsequently restaged on Atlanta Contemporary Dance Company; BEDCO

Salt Lake City Rag/Evelyn Jensen; Ames, Iowa; Iowa State University Dancers; subsequently restaged on University of Utah Ballet Ensemble; Ballet West; Pasadena (California) Dance Theatre; University of Nebraska at Omaha Dance Program

1974

Jukebox/Glenn Miller and His Orchestra; Moorhead, Minnesota; RDT; subsequently restaged on Winnipeg's Contemporary Dancers; Concert Dance Company of Boston; Dance/LA (Los Angeles); BEDCO; UNM Dance Company (two different productions)

As Quiet As/Michael Colgrass; Salt Lake City; Virginia Tanner's Children's Dance Theatre

Iris and Emily/Evans; Salt Lake City; RDT

Meditation/Leonard Bernstein; Cleveland, Ohio; Fairmount Contemporary Ballet Company

Bernstein's Mass/Leonard Bernstein; Salt Lake City; dancers chosen in open audition; Utah Symphony Orchestra

1973

Hard Times/Deseret String Band; Iowa City; Universiy of Iowa Center for New Performing Arts Dance Ensemble; subsequently restaged on RDT; Dance Gallery (Salt Lake City and Seattle); BEDCO; Atlanta Contemporary Dance Company; Concert Dance Company of Boston; Fairmount Dance Theatre (Cleveland); Chicago Moving Company; Tennessee Dance Theatre (Nashville); Raymond Johnson Dance Company (New York City)

Three Bach Dances/J. S. Bach; Lee, Massachusetts/Jacobs Pillow; Cynthia Gregory, Clark Tippet and Terry Orr (members of American Ballet Theatre)

Cambridge Dances/J. S. Bach; Cambridge, Massachusetts; Harvard Summer Dance Center Company

Within Bounds/Terry Riley; Salt Lake City; RDT; subsequently restaged on Harvard Summer Dance Center Company; Fairmount Dance Theatre; BEDCO

Solstice/Morton Subotnick; Evanston, Illinois; Gus Giordano Dance Company

Dances for King Chapel/Evelyn Jensen; Cornell, Iowa; Iowa Dance Councils Summer Workshop

Harold/Scott Joplin; Edmonton, Alberta; BESD

1972

Five Songs in August/Stanley Sussman (commissioned score); Salt Lake City; RDT; subsequently restaged on Fairmount Dance Theatre (Cleveland); Concert Dance Company of Boston; BEDCO; UNM Dance Company

Piano Rags/Scott Joplin; Salt Lake City; RDT; subsequently restaged on BEDCO

The Legacy/Harold Shapero; Salt Lake City; RDT; subsequently restaged on University of Utah Modern Dance Department; Harvard University Summer Dance Center Company; BEDCO; Winnipeg's Contemporary Dancers; Pasadena Dance Theatre

Gospel Songs/Mormon hymns; Salt Lake City; RDT Summer Workshop

1971

Tin-Tal/Mahapurush Misra; Salt Lake City; RDT; subsequently restaged on Fairmount
    Dance Theatre; BEDCO; Winnipeg's Contemporary Dancers; Chicago Repertory
    Dance Ensemble; Ruth Langridge Dance Company (San Francisco); University of
    California at Los Angeles Dance Department; Three's Company (San Diego); solo
    version—BESD; Gregg Lizenbery; Woody McGriff (Austin, Texas); Maya Ward (Santa
    Fe); Raymond Johnson (New York City)
Malcomb/Sonia Zarek; Grinnell, Iowa; Iowa Dance Councils Summer Workshop
Old American Songs/Aaron Copland; St. Louis, Missouri; Alexandra Ballet Company

1970

For Betty/Antonio Vivaldi, Salt Lake City, RDT; subsequently restaged on Concert
    Dance Company of Boston; Chicago Moving Company; Fairmount Dance
    Theatre; Maryland Dance Theatre (College Park); Virginia Tanner's Children's
    Dance Theatre; Lawton Civic Ballet Company (Oklahoma); BEDCO; University of
    Utah Modern Dance Department; Western Washington University (Bellingham);
    Chamber Dance Company (Seattle); UNM Dance Company; Dancers' Company,
    Brigham Young University
Sea Children/Claude Debussy; Salt Lake City; Virginia Tanner's Children's Dance
    Theatre

1969

Aufbrucken/Morton Subotnick; West Berlin, Germany; Deutsche Oper Ballet;
    subsequently restaged on RDT; Ruth Page's Chicago Ballet; BEDCO
Tropic Passion/Darius Milhaud; Salt Lake City; RDT

1968

Interim/Henk Badings; Salt Lake City; RDT
Bach to Bach/Norma Dalby; Salt Lake City; RDT
Chairs/a cappella; Wichita, Kansas; American Dance Symposium
Facets/Sergei Prokofiev; Lawrence, Kansas; Mid-Western Music and Art Camp;
    subsequently restaged on Virginia Tanner's Children's Dance Theatre (Salt Lake City)

1967

Dance for Three People/Eric Satie; Salt Lake City; University of Utah Department of
    Modern Dance
Lute Suite/J. S. Bach; Salt Lake City, University of Utah Department of Modern
    Dance

*These works are substantial re-workings, to the point that they constitute mostly
different choreography even though they share a title and basic concepts.
** "Evans" as the composer refers to me. "Bill Evans" as the composer refers to the world
famous jazz pianist with whom I collaborated in 1978 and 1979.

Index

Theatres

Acknowledged Individuals

I have lived a complex, rich and complete life through dance, one that has been as challenging as it has been satisfying.